AF425339

SELF-PORTRAIT

Self-Portrait

Of a Master Art Forger

A Memoir

Mark Landis

with Christen Shepherd

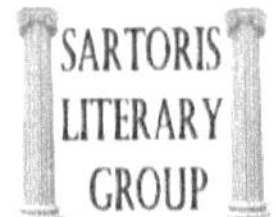

Text Copyright © 2024 Mark Landis and Christen Shepherd.

Image Copyright © 2024 Mark Landis.

ISBN: 979-8-9893644-2-8

Cover design: Mark Landis

Back Cover Photo: Khaki Plott

All rights reserved. No part of this book may be reproduced in any form without written permission from the publisher. Brief passages may be quoted in reviews. WARNING: Unauthorized duplication or downloading is a violation of applicable laws, including U.S. Copyright law. File sharing is allowed only with those companies with which Sartoris Literary Group has a written agreement.

SARTORIS LITERARY GROUP
Metro-Jackson, Mississippi
SARTORISLITERARY [DOT) com

For Dad and Mother

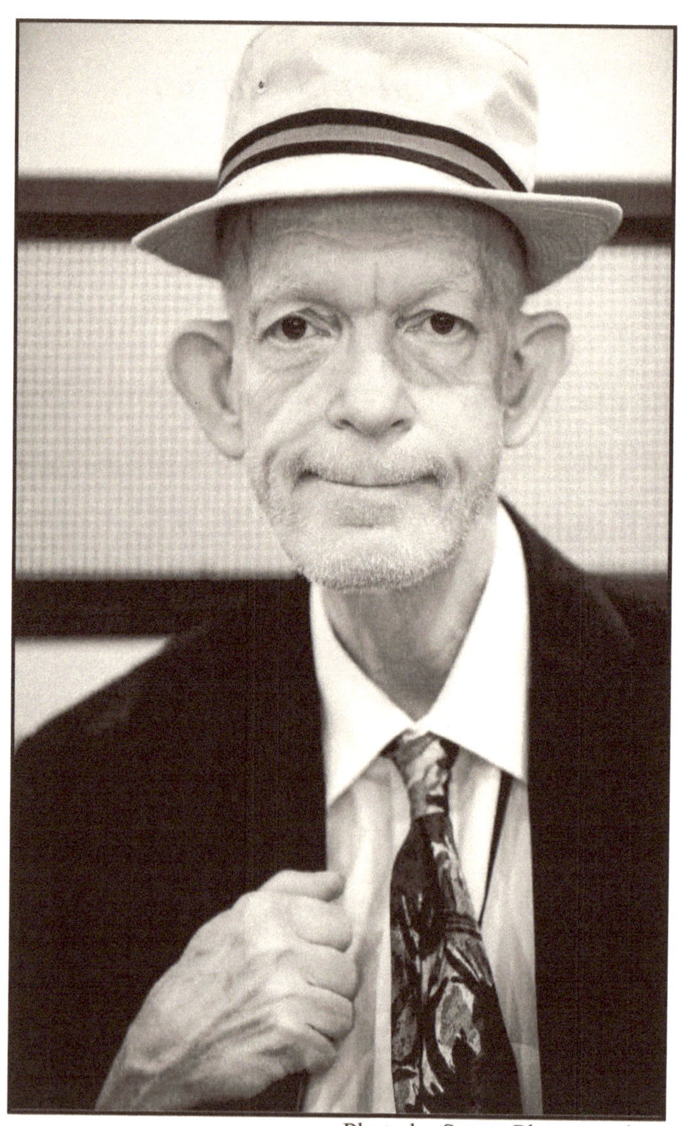

Photo by Secret Playground

Mark Landis

CONTENTS

FOREWORD

By Christen Shepherd

Truth is stranger than fiction. A diminutive man living in subsidized housing in a southern small town, posing as a wealthy philanthropist or as a Jesuit Priest, secretly begins donating masterpieces worth a small fortune. His works hang in over fifty respected American museums in twenty states until a dogged registrar at Oklahoma City Museum of Art notices a donated Paul Signac has shown up elsewhere and the jig is up. He's investigated by the FBI and goes on to become quite possibly America's most notorious art forger. Pablo Picasso, Mary Cassatt, Eagon Schiele, Maynard Dixon, Louis Valtat, and Everett Shinn, are among the varied artists Mark Landis forged and donated.

When Mark's ruse was discovered, his twenty-year hobby of "philanthropy" came to an end, as did one of the most unusual stories in the world of American art. He has never profited from any of his donated pieces, never selling them or taking a charitable receipt, and although investigated by the FBI he was never charged with a crime. The onus was on museums to verify the authenticity and thus Mark never crossed the line of breaking the law.

Numerous publications, such as *The New York Times*, covered stories about him. He is the subject of the documentary *Art and Craft*, directed by Jennifer Grausman, Sam Cullman, and co-directed by Mark Becker, which premiered in 2014 and went on to make the Oscars short-list and was nominated for an Emmy.

Mark continues to be a skilled artist, and has found other ways to connect with people through his art. He has gone on to produce works of

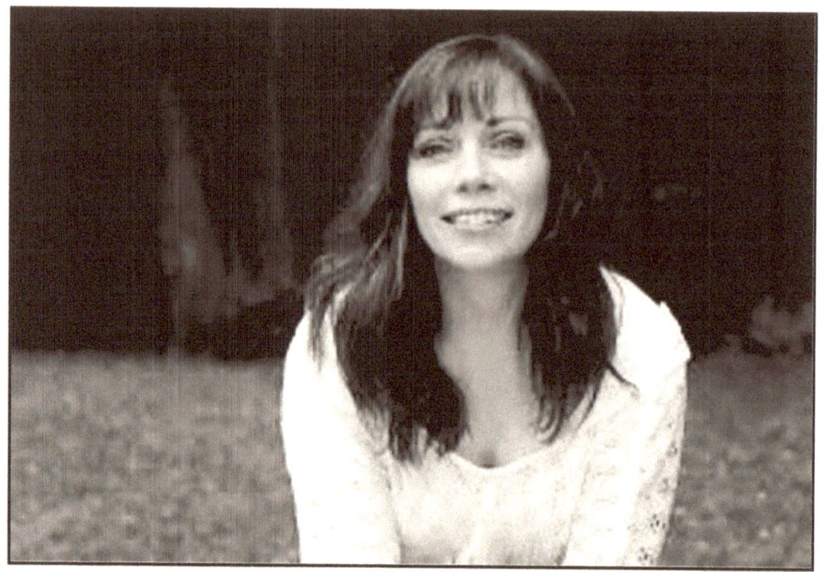

Christen Shepherd   Photo by Liana Louzon

his own, from religious icons to pastoral scenes, many of which are sold at a gallery in Laurel, Mississippi where he resides. He accepts commis - sions from time to time and has painted families and pets from photographs. Mark no longer paints forgeries, and when asked to copy a masterpiece Mark will change something about it to make that clear. Today, with his skill level only increasing, Mark is able to whip up a convincing Rembrandt or Da Vinci in a matter of days.

Recently he painted a large canvas of Emanuel Lutze's Washington Crossing the Delaware, no small feat in his tiny bedroom, the large canvas perched on an old black folding chair. On this particular piece he painted the faces of the people who'd commissioned the work in place of the men in the boat. As well, Mark painted a replica of the Salvator Mundi, the original possibly painted by Leonardo da Vinci, for the film premiere of *The Lost Leonardo.*

When he was no longer able to pose as a philanthropist Mark's true philanthropy began and he has often donated his portraits to raise money for various causes, many of which go for a large sum because of his notoriety and talent. There continues to be interest in Mark and his work, and he's frequently asked for an interview, a German podcast here, an art textbook there.

He has had exhibitions of his own, beginning in 2012 with *Faux Real*, an exhibition at the Dorothy W. and C. Lawson Reed Jr. Gallery, University of Cincinnati, where numerous forgeries collected by Matthew Leininger and Aaron Cowan were on display in an attempt to expose his work. Following that he was part of the exhibit *Intent to Deceive*, a travelling exhibit of forgeries. Most recently he has had exhibits at the Salomon Art Gallery in New York City and the Norman Rockwell Museum in Massachusetts. There is no doubt that Mark Landis will remain one of the most intriguing art forgers in modern history.

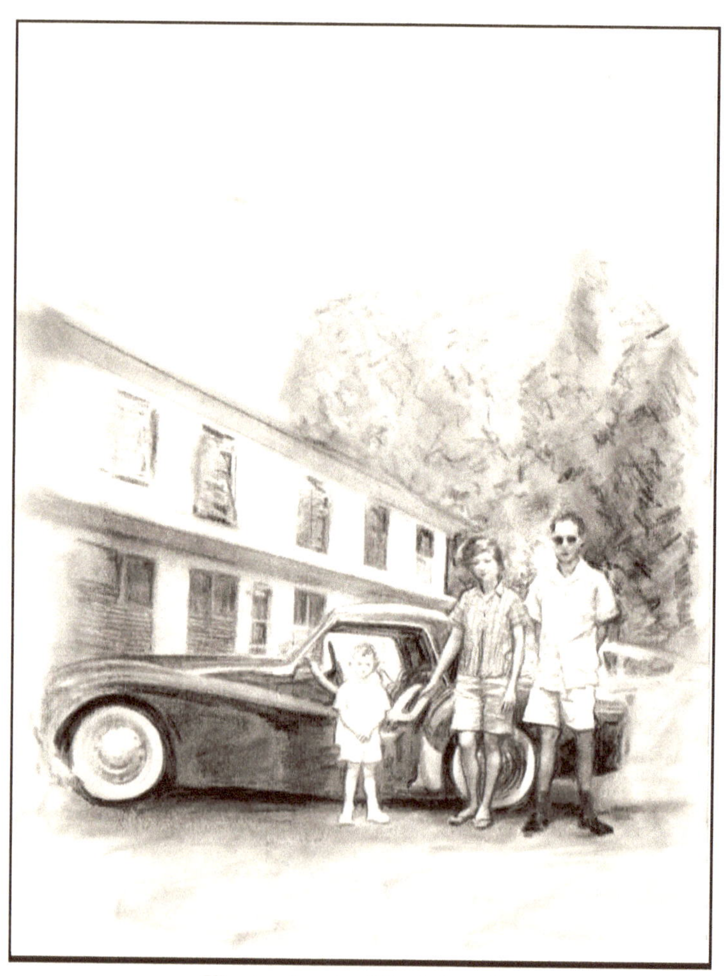

Illustration by Mark Landis

1

FAMILY

One might say my whole life was one of failure, rejection, and social humiliation, but one might also acknowledge the rather remarkable story arc that I couldn't have foreseen. While living in a group home everyone's lives were predicted by doctors, and they said I would be in institutions forever. Yet here I am, the subject of a documentary, with art exhibitions of my own, a friend to fashionable celebrities. A twist of fate, documentary filmmakers at my door, and all of this came to be.

A poem I once wrote reads:
Time and chance our lives determined,
perhaps a prayer, perhaps a sermon.

You can affect certain things in your life, but in the end, your life is determined by chance. Mine has been. I don't believe in humblebrag. So often people—celebrities especially—are proud of how modest they are, how self-deprecating—but in essence they're just proud of how humble they are. You may as well simply be proud, and I truly believe self-esteem is so important. After everything I've been through, I don't mind telling people that things turned out much better for me than professionals had envisioned.

No one seemed to have much use for me when I was younger. Dad and Mother were intelligent and attractive people, and according to the Menninger Clinic I, their only son, had a physical genetic anomaly or defect, although they decided it had nothing to do with the behaviour or psychological problems that brought me to that psychiatric hospital. Life has not been easy, and even after my notoriety not everyone has been kind. Someone once wrote about me in an article and referred to me as a

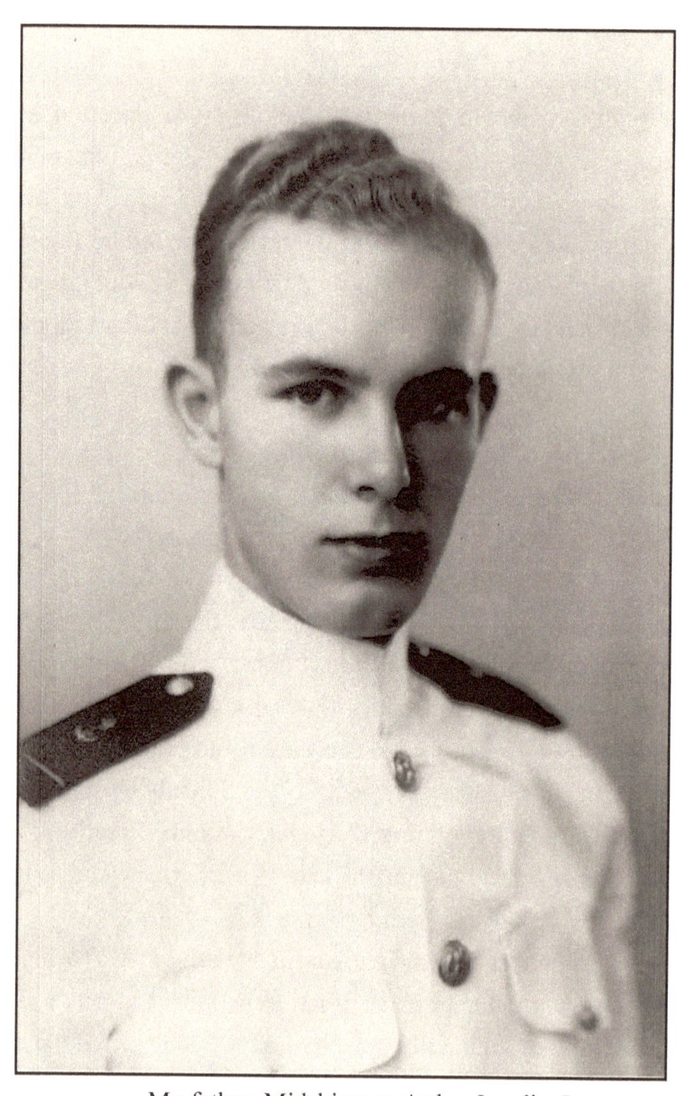

My father, Midshipman Arthur Landis, Jr.

"cadaverous little creep with the Norman Bates complex." You remember the mean things people say, but I also try and focus on the positive, and in the end the writer is rather good to me and compared me to other important artists.

There are eight million stories in the city, as they say, and they can be made interesting or not. Looking back at my life, it's easier to remember things thirty years ago than two days ago. I have a pretty accurate memory, but I never know if I've changed some facts over time because sometimes I can get creative with stories. When I was young our reception on TV was remarkably poor by today's standards, where we take clear pictures for granted and everything is in high definition. But growing up I never saw a clear picture, and maybe 80-90 percent of the time I could scarcely see anything at all, just ghosts, so I had to use my imagination. Because of that I have quite a developed imagination and I tend to embellish stories even when I don't mean to.

I once told Mother something about her family and accidentally added in some things I heard on TV, all to her own mother's benefit because the story was much more interesting, but I didn't realize I had made a large portion of it up. I tend to do that. I have saved a lot of letters and photographs through the years, so now I often look things up to be sure I'm remembering correctly.

I've read memoirs by criminals, and I certainly didn't want to write a book like theirs, boasting about how clever I am at crime and all the people I've fooled. I never wanted to be like that, proud of what I got away with, so in writing my story I just talk about my life such as it was. I've noticed very few people say much in their own autobiographies, discussing only admirable things because they are conscious of how they appear, and naturally when people are self-conscious the reader never finds out anything important. I read Miriam Gish's autobiography because I enjoyed a couple of movies she was in. I remember getting up at 11:00 PM when I was a teenager to watch one on PBS. I learned very little while reading her book, but as it turns out she was friends with Tennessee Williams. Because I usually checked out new books at the library I found myself reading his.

He had been friends with many people from the beginning of the last century until the 1950s and had interviewed them. Naturally, when people are talking to someone else, they confide things they wouldn't tell the general public or put in their own memoirs.

Miriam Gish told him that in her early years she saw her mother stealing the waiter's tips and they snuck out of a hotel without paying. Of course, had she put that in her autobiography it would have made her mother look bad, but then I found out about it anyway thanks to Tennessee Williams' honesty. What I took away from that is that when someone is writing a memoir it's human nature to not make yourself look bad, but I don't worry about what people will think of me now—I've already been in trouble—so what I've written is the truth as I see it.

People should always reflect. I made friends with a missionary and she showed me pictures of kids in Chad who have absolutely nothing. They might be born with hearing loss, or blind, and with all kinds of terrible health conditions. No TV. No one ever gives them a thought. I wouldn't have thought about them if she hadn't told me about them.

People need to reflect when they go on about their hardships around here. The way people go on about things now … they get all upset with scandals, but people elsewhere may have it much harder. We shouldn't feel sorry for ourselves. I certainly don't look back at my life and wish for things to be different. Mother and Dad were terrific to me, so I have no complaints. I am just sorry I was a disappointment.

I was born Mark Agustus Landis, on March 10, 1955, in Norfolk, Virginia. I don't know as much about my parents as some might, and I have only an inkling of how my parents may have met. In World War II the government hired a lot of young women to do things that computers do now, like filing and typing, and Mother went to work in Washington so maybe that's where they were introduced. I know she didn't go by herself, and probably went with other young ladies or perhaps my aunt. Now that Mother is gone, I have no way of finding out. She was bitter that Dad

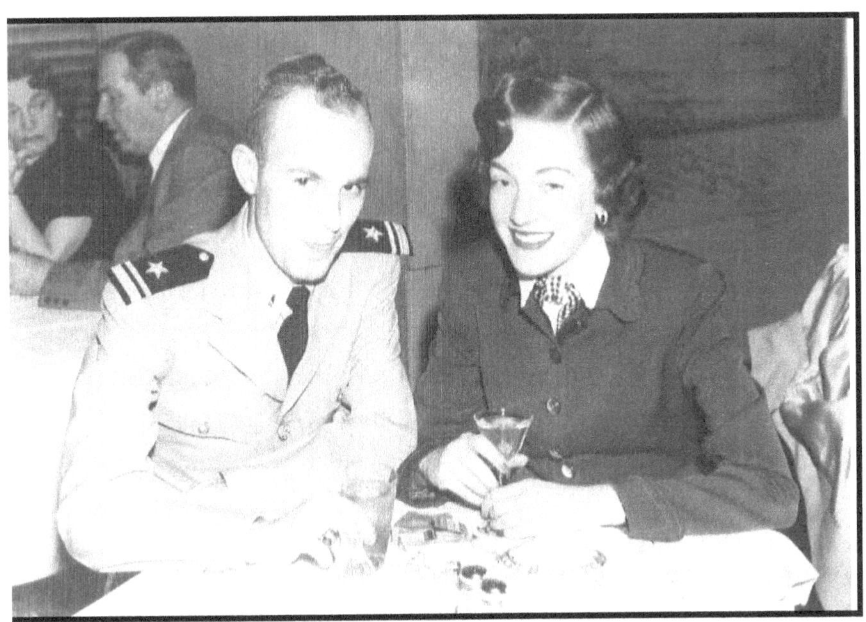

Mother and Dad as newlyweds.

didn't leave us any money when he died so, unfortunately, she didn't tell me certain things.

Tidying up during the pandemic I found an old mimeograph that I nearly threw out, but something made me glance at it, and it was a love letter from Dad to Mother when he was staying in officers' quarters. It was a typed letter, addressed "Dear Wife," and he said that he hadn't been able to write because his fountain pen was in the shop. In the second paragraph Dad says he goes to a bar to watch TV, which is what you did in the 1950s. He signed the letter, Love Knothead. I could tell he loved my mother. It was the only love letter Mother saved, and maybe only by accident because it was in Dad's papers. Over the years we traveled a lot, and they were happy for a long time.

Dad was born in New York. The pictures I have of him when he was little were taken there, but he sort of grew up in Indianapolis. He had an Andy Hardy-type childhood. He had a little Auburn speedster push pedal car when he was a boy. Grandfather was vice president of manufacturing at the Auburn car factory in the twenties, when Auburn was doing well. Their best years were 1929 and 1930. Connersville was where the plant was located. The company went under in 1937 when Dad was twelve and his brothers were much younger.

My Dad's family was the good side of the family, in the same social class as doctors, approaching upper class. Dad's brothers I didn't really know, and I never met one of them at all. I have a wonderful photograph of Dad and his family. Bachrach was one of the most prestigious photographers in the country at the time. They photographed a lot of prestigious people like Thomas Edison and Albert Einstein, and they did the photo of Grandmother and my father and uncles. My impression is they went to New York to have the picture taken.

Grandmother looks so elegant, sitting with a cocker spaniel. Dad had three brothers, Robert, the oldest and known as Bob, William who was the middle child and called Bill, and Charles, who was the youngest and called Bud. Dad was called Buster. They are all gone except Uncle Charles, whom I haven't seen since I was fourteen.

We saw a good deal of Uncle Charles and Robert when we lived in Washington D.C. because they were living there, or at least Charles was, or places near each other. Then we moved. Uncle Charles had been a smart, intelligent looking boy, and he ended up a banker and well off. The boy that buttoned his jacket wrong in the photo, he eventually became an accountant, but I never did meet him. I seemed to overhear my mother talking to other people that he borrowed money a lot from my great-aunts and had financial trouble. He was a CPA. The other brother taught most of his adult life at the Haverford School, a prestigious preparatory boys' school.

Dad was in the same class at the naval academy as President Carter. In the '90s I wrote President Carter and asked if he remembered Dad being in class with him in 1947 and he wrote me back.

I believe Dad had a sense of humour but the only way I'd know that was overhearing him with his friends. Dad graduated in 1947 and was an ensign. He was such a good-looking naval officer. As a young lieutenant

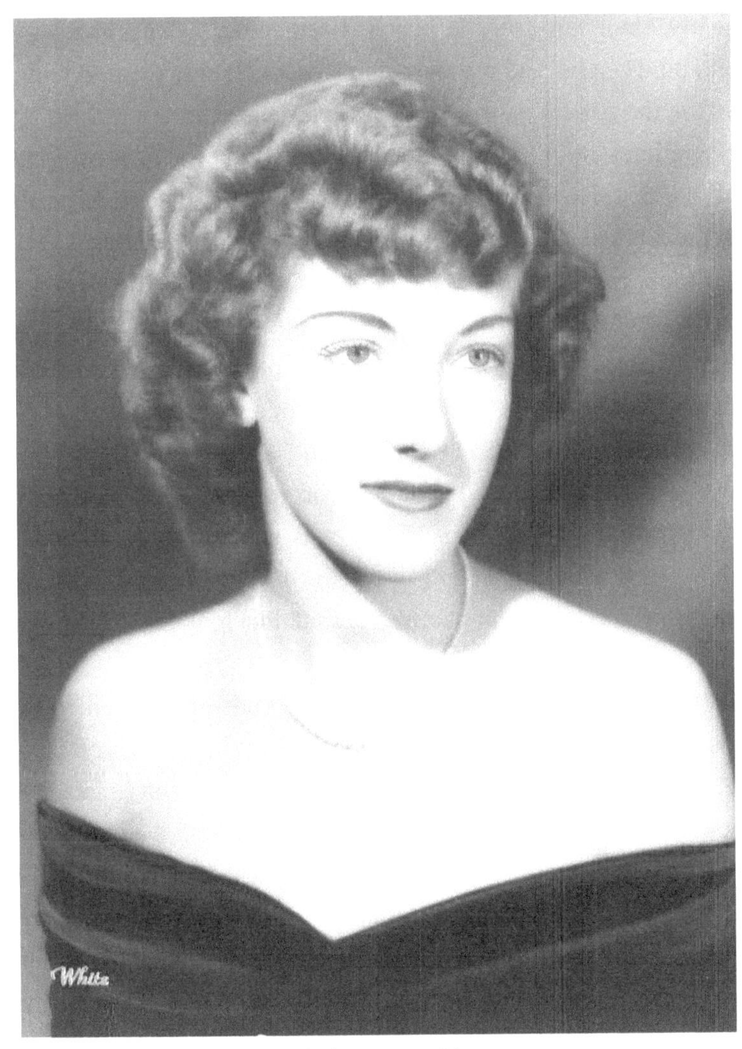

Mother at age 21.

he'd commanded a landing ship transport, known as an LST, at the Inchon Landing— which was the D Day of the Korean War. He was heroic, and he was only twenty-three. I never knew about this until fifteen years ago. Dad brought back a North Korean epaulet he took off a dead man, one of the enemy obviously, on the beach. I remember asking him about the epaulet and when he told me I was impressed. He was pleased with it. He always felt the American military was doing the right thing.

Sometimes on TV you have people saying war is awful, but Dad wasn't like that. He always hated the enemy. Other than to tell people he was in the Korean War, to other officers or friends who came to see him, he didn't talk about the details to people. Occasionally I'd overhear him talking to Mother about some fond memories. I do know there was an occasion when he was in charge where one of his sailors died. He didn't have his helmet on and one of those heavy lids slammed down and killed him. I remember overhearing Dad talking about that. It was the only casualty. I didn't talk to Dad about the Navy. I remember he would often comment on how the naval academy was sometimes an ordeal, and I wouldn't have even dared to go into it with him. I was such a disappointment to him and not athletic, so unlike him, and it just wouldn't even have occurred to me to discuss it.

I remember hearing Dad talking about a midshipman, a hero to those at the naval academy, Count von Luckner. I was awfully young when I heard Dad discussing him. The way I'd understood it, von Luckner was an old German count in World War I who wanted to join the Navy, but they told him he was too old, so he put a gun on his yacht called the Sea Adder and raided ships, sinking many of them. In 1965 Dad bought me a plastic model of the SMS Sea Adder, as well as others. He helped me assemble it but in the end he basically did it himself. In truth, the real von Luckner was just a commissioned naval officer with his ship commissioned as a raider, and frankly, he sounded like a stereotype. I recall that when I researched him he was a real disappointment.

One thing I have to say about Dad is that he was a gentleman, a real gentleman, like you'd find in the 19th century, the sort of men where if

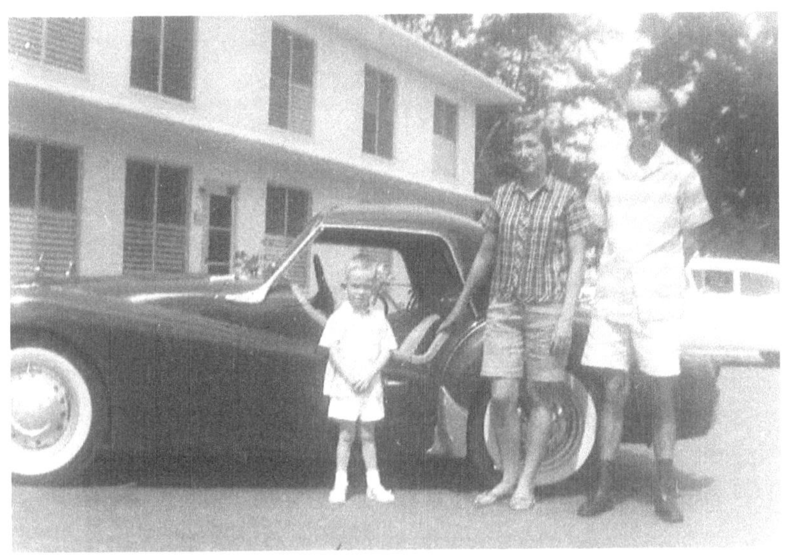

My family.

they gave someone their word they always kept it. That's why leaving the Navy was so bad for him. You have to retire from the military if you're passed over for a promotion, and he just couldn't get on afterwards. He couldn't have succeeded in any kind of business because he was simply too honest. Much like the title of the movie *An Officer and a Gentleman.* Dad was both an officer and a true gentleman, just like one should be. I didn't inherit those qualities; I'm very good at being dishonest.

People read more in Dad's generation, and he certainly read a lot, and received books in the mail. Dad's politics were very conservative, the way you'd expect for someone who worked for NATO, keeping the communists at bay and worrying about draft dodgers, and things like that; but Dad died before the scandals. Everyone like him (a career officer in the 1960s) had an opinion on everything. Mother was like me; her politics would just be the same as Dad's because she wouldn't have cared that much. I can't understand why people get so political and so upset and get into arguments, but then I can't understand why people go crazy over football games. I guess at least with politics it will have some effect on me, but how could a football game possibly hurt me? People tend to get far too overwrought about such things.

I believe Mother liked Dad's side of the family. His parents died before Mother met them, so she never had complaints about mothers-in-law like they do on TV. I had great-aunts on Dad's side, sisters of Grandfather, named Augusta, Florence, and Gertrude. Aunt Augusta was a strong, opinionated woman, and she went to one of those American women's colleges around 1900. She travelled a great deal before the First World War.

Apparently, my aunts were all young women who wanted to do things. They liked to travel. I didn't know Aunt Gertrude but she sounded quite admirable. She became a missionary, and she went to China. She brought back a nice Mah Jong set and a Pekingese syllabary, full of helpful Chinese phrases dated 1914, and I still have them both. She also brought back a disturbing print of unbaptized Chinese babies crying and burning in a fire in Hell. It was creepy, and it later disappeared. I liked the picture because teenage boys are like that, but Mother didn't. I noticed when I came back from the Menninger Clinic and I stayed with Mother for two weeks until I went to the Chicago Art Institute that she had gotten rid of it, which means she gave it away to a rummage sale or something. She was in a small apartment at that point because, as she put it, "Dad left us nothing."

Aunt Augusta is whom Mother knew best. She was quite elderly, but I had to go visit her. I know Dad didn't want to go either, but you have to visit family when they are older and lonely. Life imitates TV and TV plagiarizes life. I did find myself enjoying the time we spent with Aunt Augusta, and she took an interest in me. Adults sometimes pretend they will leave you money so you'll take an interest in them. She would drop hints, and I think Mother hoped she would leave them money, but in the end she didn't leave us anything. I certainly didn't blame her—it got her company. It's similar to what I did by donating paintings so I would have friends. Loneliness and poor self-esteem made me donate. I don't expect people to visit me.

Aunt Augusta put herself on a plane and came down to see Dad when he was dying. She was in her early seventies. She was relatively well off as she'd married a banker when she was sixty, and I believe she helped my uncle financially, (the brother who didn't button his coat right in the family picture.) He had a big family and had financial troubles. I never met all those cousins.

I didn't know Aunt Gertrude—I met her once in a nursing home but she was too far gone to get to know her. Dad's brothers didn't visit him when he was ill, but they called him. In those days a long-distance call was expensive, so you'd notice it.

My mother, she uplifted herself, a lot like the movie *The Heart is a Lonely Hunter,* which Mother and I watched on the screen coming from Europe by ship in 1968. She got us into first class so we were able to see a showing at a convenient time. It's an important movie to me and made quite an impression. I can watch it over and over. Mother's name was Jonita, but a lot of people called her Jo.

Mother's family was kind of the bottom of the social ladder, on the lower rungs but not the lowest. If you knew Mother you'd never know she was from Mississippi. When I came back from San Francisco after my nervous breakdown (which is just a euphemism for all kinds of things), they were taking care of my grandmother after my grandfather died and I couldn't believe I was related to them. I'd met my grandmother when we lived in Washington and we took the train to see her. I remember they left me at the Laurel Public Library because they were going shopping. I saw the core collection from the founders at that time because the gallery was attached to the library.

Mother had one sister and one brother. Mother was the eldest and I believe she was closest to her sister, Gloria who was two years younger. Uncle Rodney is still alive and in his eighties, the only relative I'm in communication with, as he is in charge of my trust. I send him things and maybe see him once a year, and he's good about keeping me up to date on things by email, although I'm not particularly close to him.

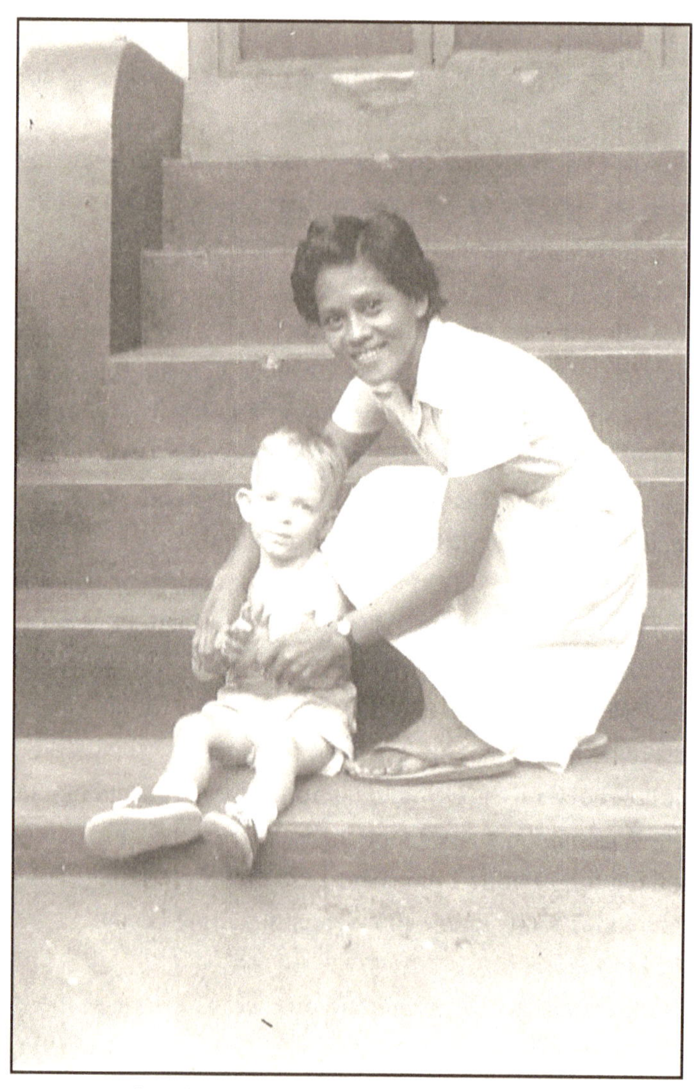

In the Philippines with our *au pair*, Connie.

As a teenager Mother went to secretarial school, an honourable position in those days. They had a national secretary day. Nowadays you can't refer to someone as a secretary; it's a "personal assistant," or they get offended. Mother started out as a filer or secretary. My guess is she really worked hard and uplifted herself, and probably by watching movies and being around girls form other parts of the country she completely lost her accent. A lot of people didn't have TV in the 1950s, so that's why I assume she learned to talk the way she did—by watching movies. She thought her family sounded like *the Beverley Hillbillies.*

Yet, *s*ometimes, Mother would almost sound like Mrs. Drysdale on *the Beverly Hillbillies* and then would slip into a royal way of speaking, although we didn't even have money. Mrs. Drysdale was a bit like Mother, pretentious but didn't have anything to be pretentious about. My grandmother's house was a tacky place. Mother had a wealth of antique furniture collected in the U.K. and France, and she had excellent taste, always trying to uplift herself and me, too.

When Dad was stationed in Manila they travelled a lot and they got much of their furniture there, all made of beautifully carved wood, and we had a beautiful musical table Mother and Dad got in Venice, and when you lift the lid and wind it, it plays music.

Mother would have all that expensive furniture in my grandmother's modest house, but Mother pretended it was a palace. People came for dinner and she'd set a table and put out linen and silver and expensive chargers, like something out of Emily Post. People liked Mother and thought she was nice. Harriet McGibbon, who played Mrs. Drysdale, could have played my mother in a movie. You can get an impression of mother if you see Harriet McGibbon in the bank examiner episode of the Beverly Hillbillies, or in the Tennessee Williams play *A Caged Bird*—she was like the mother in that. Most of all I think of the *Beverly Hillbillies* episode with Mrs. Drysdale, called the Art Center, Season 3, number 34. It is there that she most reminds me of my mother.

I'm sure my grandmother liked her other grandchildren better than me. She wasn't polite and she'd say the N word. One relative was like a character on television, like the girlfriend of the boy who holds up convenience stores on *In the Heat of the Night*. I caught her red-handed stealing Mother's jewellery when Mother was sick. She was going through the jewellery and when she saw me she pretended she was helping and said, "What jewellery will your mother want at the hospital?" It was absurd to think that Mother needed it there.

Mother's family wasn't as good as Dad's, and that's why she knew what was going on with me with the art forgeries but didn't say anything. She liked getting the letters from the bishop. She was like a lot of us … you want to feel important. She took friends from her bridge club to see the picture I did hanging in the Lauren Rogers Museum, and she spoke about me in unrealistic ways when I wasn't around.

There are some rules where if you break them it's fine to look the other way, but if there was really something she thought was wrong she'd get really mad and yell. If I had to leave really early for the airport, like at three or four in the morning, she'd get up, because people Mother's age are always dull in terms of worrying about things, and she'd fear the doors wouldn't be properly secured so she'd see me off.

She was not an affectionate lady, but we were close. We could read each other's mind. When there were problems with my stepfather she'd look at me and we'd think the same thing. We were co-conspirators, cronies. I've been able to lie to a lot of people, but I could never lie to her. She just always knew.

Mother had ideas about what was "common," and everything had to be aristocratic. If there was the least suspicion something might be common she didn't approve of it. We had au pairs, an Australian girl named Wendy and a French one who would watch me if Mother and Dad would go to Monaco. There were certain high class card games we had to play, ones she perceived were upper class or more refined, even if we struggled, and I don't think even Mother understood some of them. She was really good at bridge, but the game requires four people. Mother and Dad had a travelling card set they got in Italy, and it's older than I am. We played two French card games.

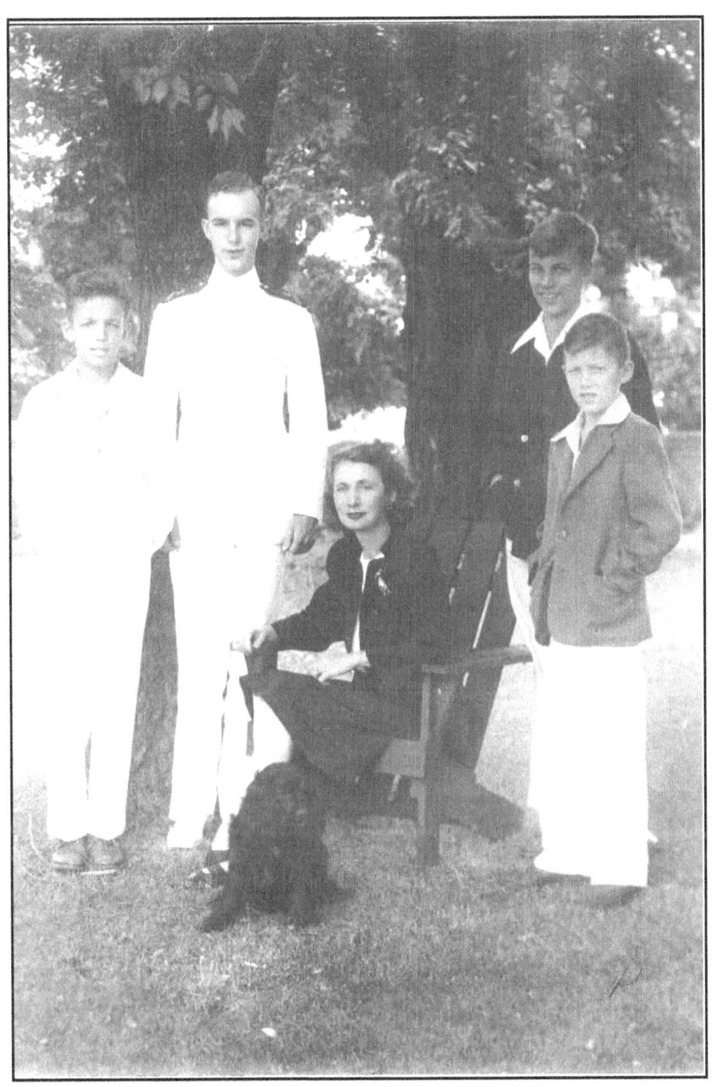

Grandmother, Dad, second from left, and my uncles.

I'd sometimes overhear her talking about her travels to people. I know on the Riviera they saw a lot of celebrities. She spoke of seeing Princess Grace and Prince Rainier, and it's quite possible Mother and Dad were in a reception line and got to meet them, but I just don't know. Mother always wore a charm bracelet, and she collected things to represent places where she'd lived or visited so she could show people and talk about it. The little boy, the Manneken Pis, from Brussels, the little mermaid from Copenhagen, the Eiffel tower, a matador, a fan from the Philippines and Manila, Japanese gates, a wooden shoe, Maltese crosses.

When I was in San Francisco I wanted to get Dad's Hamilton watch repaired and went to a jeweller who was a friend of Mr. Torres. I ended up buying a charm of a streetcar, and I gave it to Mother for a gift. I think it cost $100, which was a lot of money for me at the time. When she received it she said, "I don't want this charm with the common charms" and she wouldn't put it on her bracelet. It was special to her, so she kept it separate and wore it as a pendant.

My parents were good to me, but I had no confidence in myself. Why did I have poor self-esteem? How do you say it without using a blunt instrument? I was a disappointment to Dad. I know in situation comedies the dads always want boys—they come in with baseball mitts—but Dad wasn't like that, and he likely would have preferred to have had a daughter. I know if he had a son he would have liked to have had a teenage son like they have on situation comedies; they're not perfect, they get into the kind of jams you'd expect, like Bud on *Father Knows Best*. They don't do drugs or steal cars, they just have trouble with girlfriends, like, *Gee, I made two dates for the prom, now what do I do?* Always standard plots for teenagers, over and over with variations. Meanwhile, I was in my room all the time, didn't have any friends, and certainly didn't have any girlfriends. Dad would have liked a son that got into the troubles that mainly Wally and Beaver may have gotten into, those typical themes.

The last time dad took interest in me was London. I was twelve … and after that nothing. Even when I got into some kind of trouble at school he didn't do much, even if I deserved being yelled at or lectured, but he just didn't. He'd lost interest. In truth, he couldn't ground me because I just stayed in my room anyhow, but he didn't even get angry at me anymore. He did give me golf clubs once when I was a teenager. He wanted me to get into golf, but then he got sick and died so we never used them.

As a child I didn't do many foolish things but every so often I did something any child would do. It was instilled in me to not break things. I do believe I broke an ivory cigarette case. It was round and had a crown it rested on, but I was little and I broke it off. I may also have dented my little silver christening bowl. I was always warned about rings on the furniture—Mother was fanatical about such things—and I can recall this from my earliest memories. If I ever did leave rings, I would have been so young I can't remember.

You'll never hear me a say a bad word because Mother would have gotten hysterical. Mother was always the hysterical one; she'd get upset over all kinds of things, but then calm down all of a sudden. Even though she might cry and go into hysterics, Mother never ever hit me.

Dad was such a good-looking young man. He even made friends with a movie star when he was a cadet in the Naval Academy. She was Carol Landis, a beautiful and glamorous actress who was a huge star in the 1940s. He wrote her a letter asking if they were related because they had the same last name. She wrote back and said they couldn't be related because the studio had chosen her name. They continued writing letters and "Aunt Carole" sort of adopted Dad as a younger brother. He saved them in a scrapbook, and I still have the collection of letters. One thing Dad would be proud of me for, is for making friends with the famous actress Rosanna Arquette. He never got to find out about that, but he'd be pleased.

Once people started writing articles about me, I started reading things about myself, like that my ears stick out. I don't remember being teased about it much as a teenager. I was teased about other things, but not specifically my ears. I do remember one time a lady looked at a picture of me in my school uniform for St Mary's Town and Country School and I

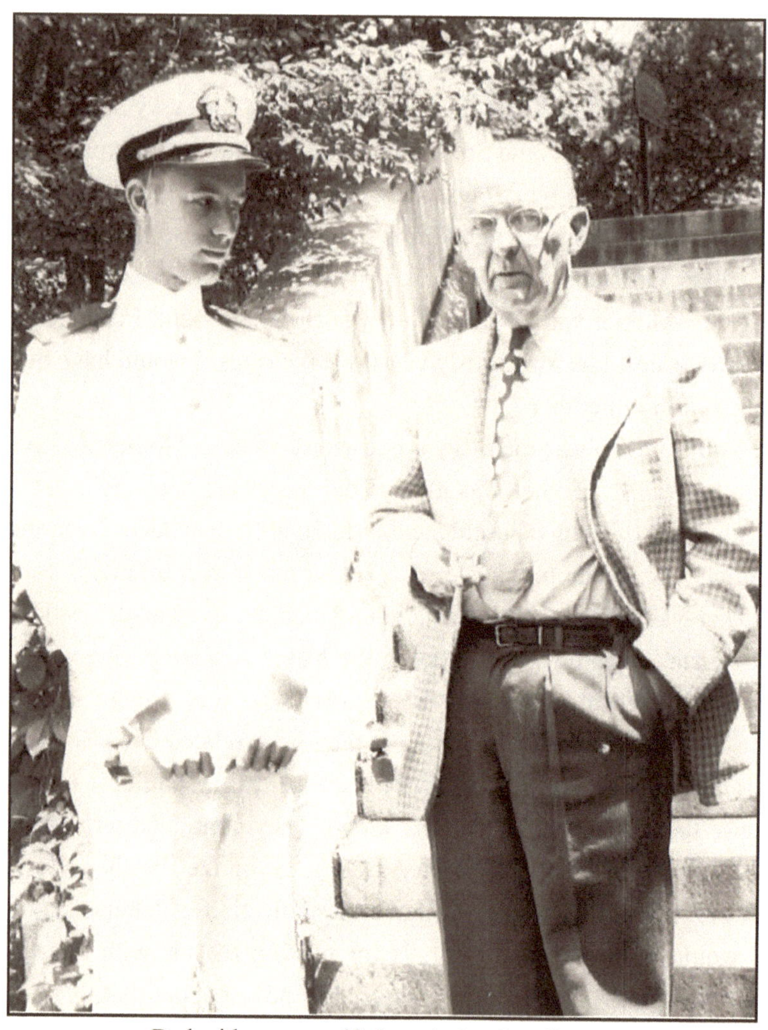

Dad with my grandfather, Arthur Landis, Sr.

remember her laughing at my ears. She made an enemy of me that day and Mother wasn't happy either.

I once overheard Mother telling one of her friends that when I was a baby I could have had my ears corrected but my father wouldn't allow it for some reason, maybe because he thought it would help me build character. When I heard this I was shocked. I've never told anyone this, but I was really mad at my father. I thought, *Gee Dad, I was a disappointment to you but you could have at least helped a little.* Today I would reprimand him for it. I might have been a little more confident. I wouldn't have known about this if I didn't listen in on conversations.

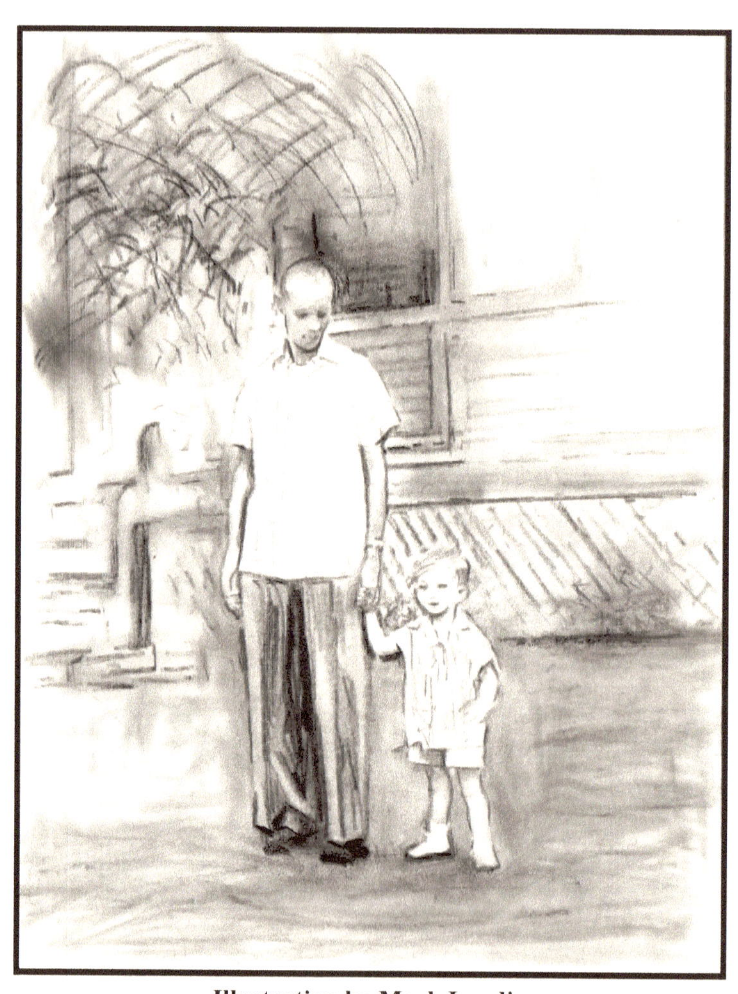

Illustration by Mark Landis

2

THE PHILIPPINES AND FRANCE

My earliest memory is at around age four or five, in the Philippines in the late 1950s. I went to nursery school from 1958 to 1959 at the U.S. naval station at Stangley point in the Philippines. My kindergarten graduation diploma says 1959.

I remember Mother talking about an incident involving me in the Philippines, speaking of it like she was amused, but she wasn't at the time. We didn't have TV but we'd go to the officers' club on the weekend and they would show movies. I remember seeing a Disney movie which we watched out on the lawn where they'd set up a screen outside. The movie had a witch or wizard in it, and after seeing that I got all of Mother's make-up and I poured it into my toy chest.

Mother and Dad were taking a nap at the time, which they did in the afternoons in Manila. In the late 1950s there were no air conditioners, or they weren't common, and we certainly didn't have one in our house—only big ceiling fans—so people took naps in the heat of the day. When Mother discovered the mess she was furious. I believe Dad did spank me for that, which I deserved. Spanking was accepted practice in those days. Mother and Dad were good to me, but sometimes you had it coming. They thought it was funny a funny story years later.

I remember Connie, the au pair. She had a no-good husband, which unfortunately, was her downfall. He drank dad's scotch, and she poured ginger ale in it to make up the difference. Dad found out and they let her go. It was quite a scene and she was quite upset about it. We also had a house boy named Chris, who was quite nice. We weren't rich, although Mother and Dad did live beyond their means, but everyone in those situations in the Philippines in the 1950s had servants.

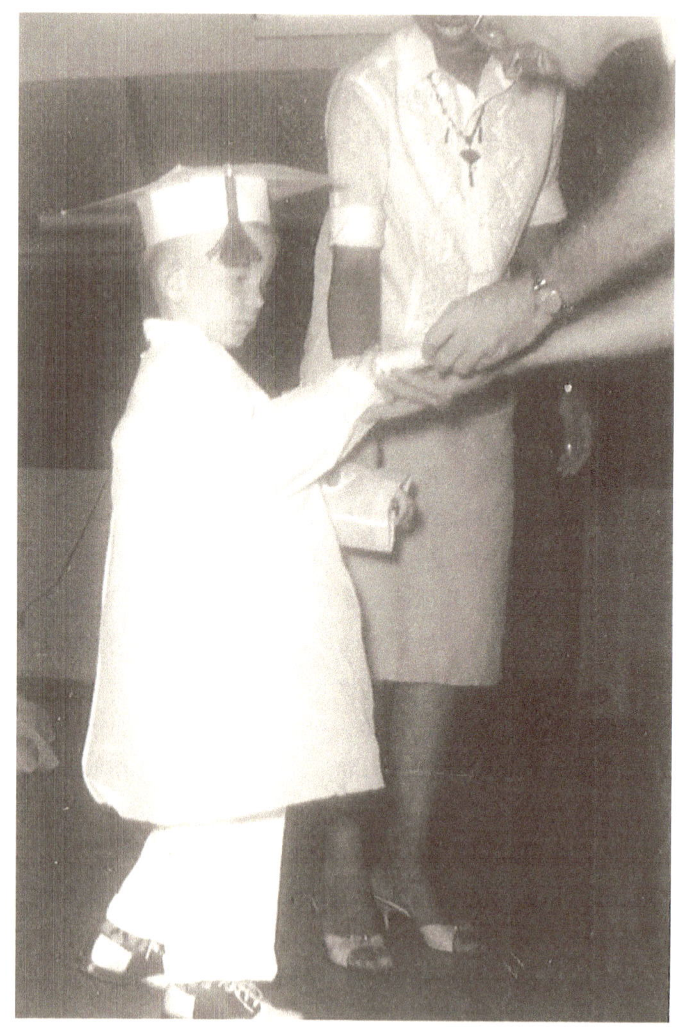

Graduation Day: Kindergarten in the Philippines.

From time to time, Mother would try her hand at artistic endeavours. In 1950 Mother painted a white magnolia flower which still hangs on our apartment wall. She enjoyed her hobby painting in the Philippines, but she wasn't very good.

We returned to the US on a ship called the SS President Cleveland in 1959 coming back from the Philippines. My debut as a stand-up comic would have been then; there's a photo of me in a sharp little suit standing at a microphone on the ship heading over, telling a joke.

Mother and Dad didn't take all of their stuff on every move through the years. Of course, they accumulated a lot and it started in the Philippines. They bought a lot in Hong Kong. The Navy was quite good about all they collected, and in Brussels the movers were there several days carefully packing things. Much of our furniture has been in the family forever, like a table Mother posed beside in her wedding photo. They moved that around a lot and I still have it.

We were back in the US for about seven or eight months, but it was practically the full term for fourth grade. We were briefly in Long Beach, California, and I guess from there we went to France. That's when I remember Mother and Dad taking me to Disneyland, just before we went overseas. I would have been awfully young, and I liked it very much. I don't believe they had complicated things like roller coasters. I might have been on a Ferris wheel one time prior, but I've never been on the big rides you see nowadays.

I didn't see an awful lot of my parents when I was young. In 1962 we went to a fashionable town in France, Saint Jean Cap Ferrat. As an adult I painted this area and it was Mother's favorite painting. Dad was communications officer for the 7th Fleet, so he'd be away on a cruiser and then we'd go meet him when he'd come in on the ship. It would dock and they'd send a launch for us so we could visit him onboard the ship and we'd have dinner together. They showed movies there, and that's where I saw *Dr. No.* They made a movie once on that ship, a pirate movie, and they sunk it for the film. For a long time you could still see the mast sticking out at Saint Jean.

There was a French au pair girl when I was very young and her downfall was that she was simply a typical teenager. Mother and Dad were young and always going out. I remember Mother lecturing the girl and telling her to stay in the house and mind me, but naturally she took me down to see her friends anyway after my parents left. Then she'd forget about me. I remember when Mother lectured her, us looking at each other while she was nodding and saying, "Oh I won't do it again," but as we exchanged glances I could tell she wouldn't stop. She knew she wouldn't obey, and of course, we left the house. I remember seeing Dad coming down the steps and finding us and I knew that would be the end of her.

The girl who was with us in London, Francois, was relatively responsible, unlike the French au pair. Mother and Dad were always doing things in London. Francois promised to take me to mass on Sundays and we went once but then went to see her boyfriend. I never told on her. She was yelled at by Mother from time to time for little things, but she was an emotional girl and if she didn't get her way she'd make a scene.

I attended an Anglo-American school, as I would again in Belgium. I still have my report card from Grade 2. Out of sixty-three term days I was absent for fourteen of them and tardy for three. I earned B's, C's and D's. My only A was in art. The teacher said, "Mark is very interested in drawing and painting and has done some excellent work."

In terms of the other subjects, the teacher described me as "careless" and said I could "do better if he wanted to." She felt that I couldn't focus but did learn easily. Apparently, I didn't always behave. The teacher's thoughts on my class conduct: "At times Mark can behave very well. During the first part of the term he was good but lately he has been very naughty."

While living in France we went to Italy. I've always copied catalogues. The earliest memory I have of copying catalogues was when we stayed at a nice hotel in Venice, like a palazzo, and another one in Florence. Mother and Dad did a real tour of Italy. We'd go to museums in the day and pick up handbooks, and I remember copying pictures out of

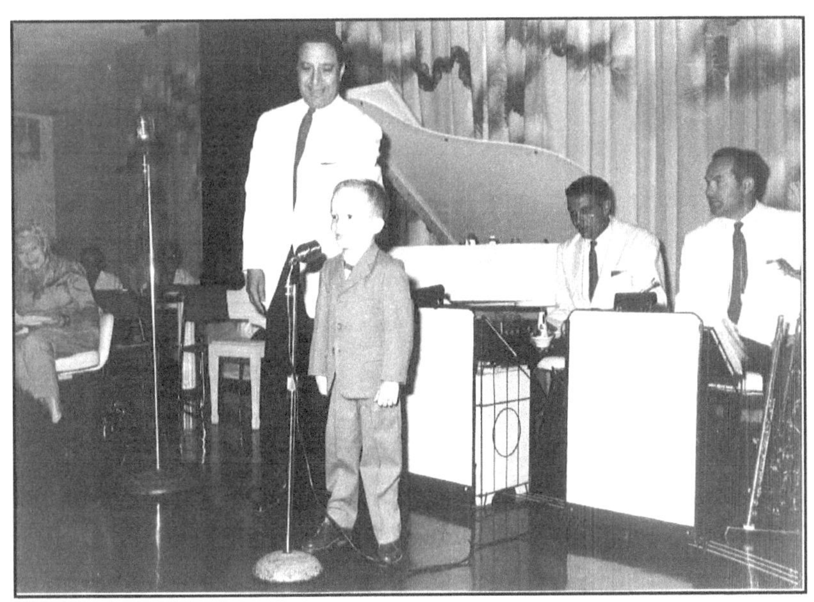

My stand-up debut on board the SS President Cleveland.

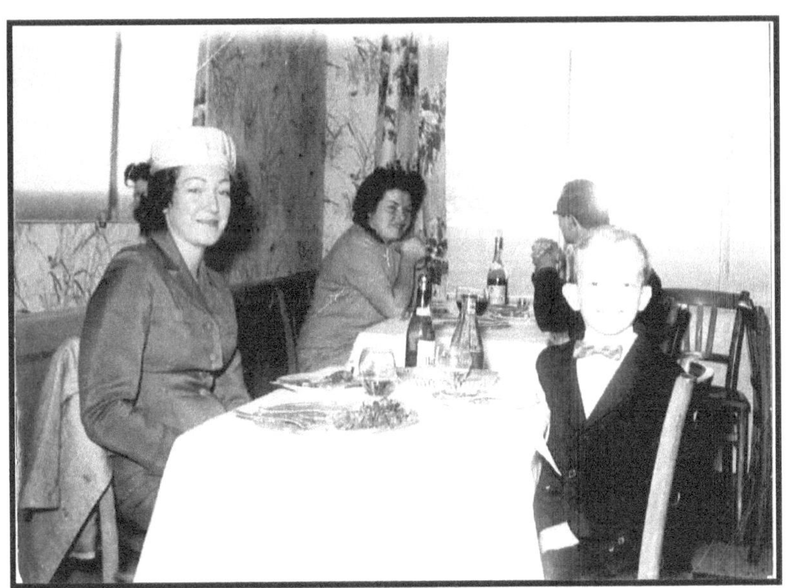

With Mother at a restaurant in Paris.

them. Sometimes I was with Mother and Dad during the day or with their friends, but I was alone a lot too in the hotel at night, which is how I got adept at copying. Even so, when I was a very young boy I didn't think of being an artist. I'm sure I'd have wanted to be something any boy would, like a secret agent, or an inspector at Scotland Yard.

We were in France until 1964. When we were in Europe we took many holidays and I remember trips to Germany, Holland, and Paris. One of the perks of Dad's working with NATO was nice hotels. I remember seeing Navy ships at the dock when we went there, but I can't remember if they were Dad's ships. In Naples we went to the pier. I think Dad must have been working then, but sometimes we were on holiday. I recall being snowed in somewhere in the Pyrenees.

Dad's ship was probably coming to Portugal or Spain. You wouldn't think of Spain as a place to get snowed in, but we did. Mother would travel with another young Navy wife, who was just young and had no children. They were friends. It would have been a little too courageous for Mother to drive alone, but she did indeed drive in snow. I remember us driving in the snow until we couldn't get any farther. Eventually we got to the port city. Mother and Dad got me a box of toy bull fighters and it was a nice little set. We went around various places in Spain.

We may have come back from the Riviera on a prop plane. I remember being on a Trans-Atlantic flight on a TWA plane with propellers, like on "I love Lucy" when Lucy was smuggling a big wheel of cheese and Lucy pretends it's her baby. Flying was nice in those days. They wouldn't hire just anybody to be a stewardess; you had to be glamorous. You also had to sign a weight contract, and I don't think you could be over 120 lbs.

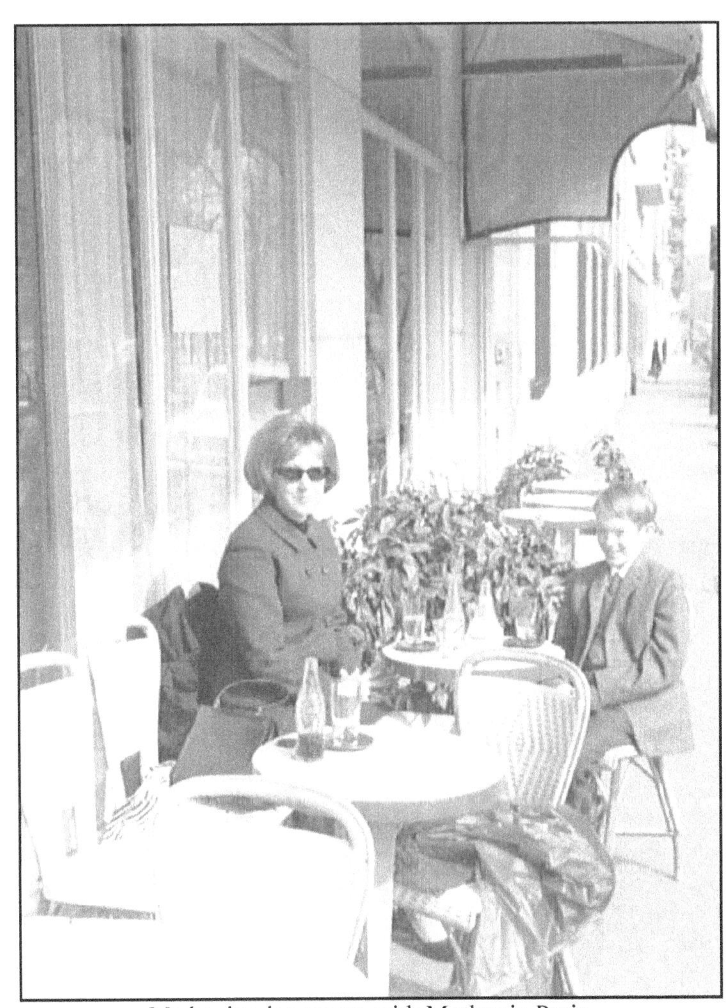

Me having ice cream with Mother in Paris.

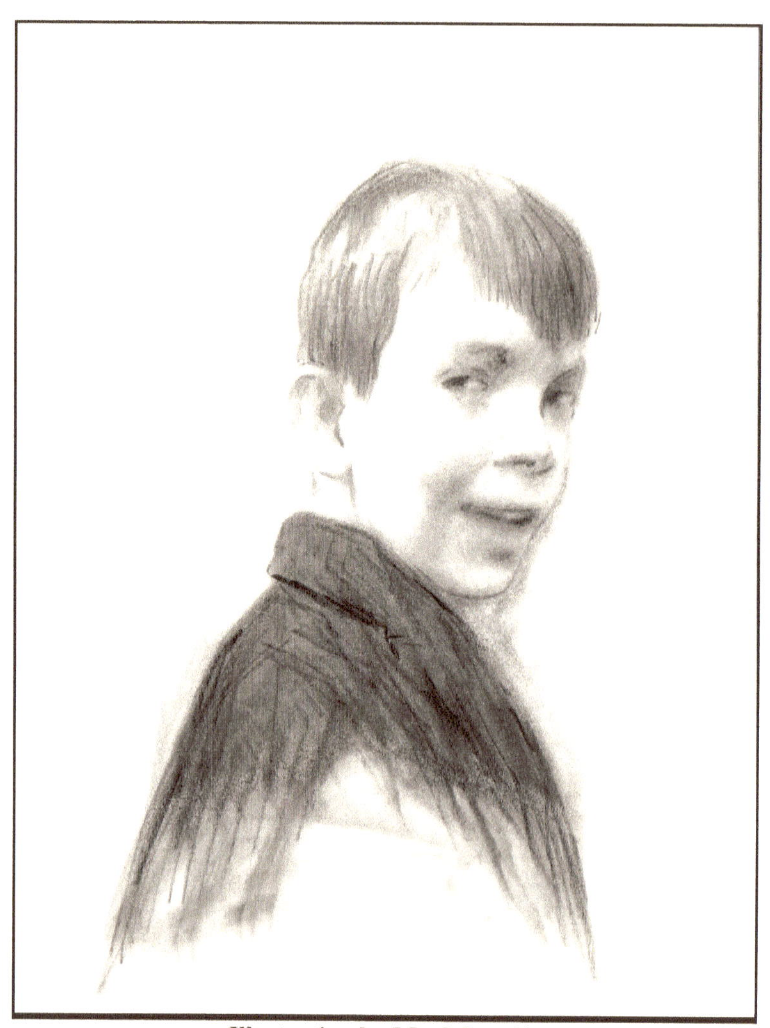

Illustration by Mark Landis

<u>**3**</u>

LONDON

We went back to the U.S. for six to eight months in 1964 before Dad's Naval posting to London, and that's when I watched TV for the first time. He was posted at a Maryland Naval base called Cheltenham, near Washington, where he worked as a communications officer. We often went into Washington on weekends. We were living in Maryland when President Kennedy was assassinated, and that's perhaps why I was so obsessed with TV shows in the 1960s, because it offered us an opportunity to laugh and we needed that.

On Saturday mornings I'd get up and watch cartoons. That's how my Saturdays always began. I watched a lot of television. I watched *The Flintstones* when it was a network show. The nicest parents I ever saw on TV were the Andersons. I've seen a lot of situation comedies, but they were the best parents.

To this day I still wonder about things I watched back then. In those days the family would get together to watch TV in the evening, and we'd schedule around the TV guide. It was the 50th anniversary of World War I at that time and they had a great documentary series on PBS that I do recall watching, called *The Great War*. It was twenty-six episodes that aired in 1964, narrated by Robert Ryan. I remember watching that with Dad and Mother. It was a ritual every Sunday night and a fond memory.

Dad probably thought I was too young to appreciate it, but he would make commentary on it, and tell me facts or give his opinions. That was Dad's favorite war; he was always reading about it, so I read a lot about it so I could please him. I remember struggling in junior high reading a book on the subject.

I joined the Boy Scouts in those days. I recall I was supposed to get promoted at the ceremony, to whatever the next level was. Although I hadn't completed what was required for the badges, I had just signed my father's signature saying that I had. I was all set to attend when Dad told me that I couldn't go. He didn't yell or hit me, but said, "You aren't going to the ceremony and you know why," and that shamed me.

Dad was a gentleman and honest. In all fairness to me, the other children had dads to help them with all those crafts and things. But I don't blame Dad. I didn't want to do all that stupid stuff myself, and if I was responsible for a ten-year-old I still wouldn't want to do it. He didn't like doing those things and neither did I. I only wanted the badges because the other boys were getting them. When I think about this incident, I realize that I started forging things at an early age.

An admiral asked Dad where he wanted to go and London was fashionable and so we moved. I remember my au pair at the time had ping pong earrings and Swinging Sixties outfits. I remember sitting there in London with Mother and Dad watching shows together, like Dad's favorite in the UK, *Till Death Do Us Part*. I watched *The Defenders* with my parents. It was about defence attorneys for the disadvantaged or wrongly accused. There is nothing new under the sun in terms of plots. *Arrest and Trial* in the 1960s and *Law and Order* are just the same. Basic plots over and over.

I went to St. Mary's Town and Country School on Eton Avenue in London, England. Mother and Dad were thinking of a more traditional type of all-boys school, but Mother liked St. Mary's better and I'm quite sure that I was happier there than I would have been otherwise. We watched a show called *St Trinian's* in the UK, which Dad liked, and my school was very much like the one on the show. It was a progressive private school for people in arts and entertainment. The parents were generally artistic types. Paul Robeson, the acclaimed Black singer and actor, had a daughter who went to my school before my time, back in the 1930s.

I was there for the upper fourth and lower fifth. You got your long pants when you're twelve and I got mine in 1966, upper fourth form. The school consisted of three big red brick Victorian buildings. I didn't board there but I did get to eat there. Fridays were bangers and mash at lunch and that was always the best meal they served. We used the ballroom for assemblies and we'd all sit on the floor while the teacher talked to us.

It was a good school and definitely inclined towards the arts and languages. I remember doing math at St. Mary's. This was in the days before we used the decimal systems, the old days of shillings and pence, and when they did move to the decimal system they could just do quick division. To teach us French, they asked each one of us to go out of the room and come back to guess the chosen noun from clues. We called it "the symbol secret" because of an advertising campaign on TV.

I had some good friends at that school. I went to St. Mary's for about two years. I was used to adjusting to different places, since we moved almost every year of my life. Of course, it would have been difficult the first few weeks but it's like that for all children.

I picked up a British accent and it still comes up a bit here and there and in my spelling, where I might spell center with an "re" instead of "er" and in the word 'theatre' rather than 'theater.' I did spell color with an "or," and not an "our," because color with a "u" sounds French. You can see photos of the school through the ages online. I was in the 1960s group, 1966-1967. Melanie was an older girl that I remember. She's posted a lot of pictures and has taken an interest in the site. We weren't friends, but I do remember her and she was nice.

Georgina Pert is the only one whose surname I remember. People always remember the ones who cause the most trouble, so no one remembers Georgina but me because she was so polite with excellent manners. When I speak to former classmates they've forgotten her. I sat next to her on an outing, and I think she was from Manchester. I remember in arts and crafts class, one little boy put chewing gum in my hair, and she was sorry for me and she said it was mean and then cut it out for me. She was a good little friend to me. She's been forgotten by others just because she was a well-behaved little girl.

In 1966 in London we still had old pound Sterling and pence, and we had eccentric teachers. No one came up better than Dickens for eccentric characters because there are so many in England. One teacher had a bad looking Beatles wig … Mr. Neville would really yell, and he could bring anyone to tears. Our class could be mischievous, and I remember people cheating. He didn't hit anyone, and he kind of knew better not to overdo it yelling at the girls. He must have made a few cry, but he mainly focused on boys. He'd yell, "You stupid, stupid boy!" He did it to everyone and made everyone cry eventually, myself included. It didn't mean anything, and we got over it right away.

My friend Peter always got yelled at for being messy and Mr. Neville could never read his writing. On a trip to the science museum there was an African exhibit and we got a lecture from Mr. Neville to the boys to not snigger. He didn't have to worry about me because Mother gave me a lecture in Europe about nudity. Mr. Neville was crazy and eccentric but he was a good and kind man and a dedicated teacher. He was just playing his part, so I have no bad feelings toward him. He dominated assemblies and directed the Christmas pageant. He was in the closet for being gay, but I didn't know that at the time. Another teacher protected him. She had lived in Germany and knew about persecution.

Mr. Neville took us for swimming lessons and it was there that I learned how to swim. Our teacher, Mr. Tolstoy taught us Geography. He took us out for soccer and cricket. He was an elegant man and much admired. I never knew why but for some reason he made us memorize the London tube system and we had to draw a map of it. We had a well-spoken teacher who taught us English composition and she got mad at the class after a scandal that involved cheating. She didn't yell at us at all, but she really shamed us. I once did a German competition and won a prize—a book called *Shifta*—and I think a teacher named Miss Haak gave it to me. I ended up giving it to the de Grummond Collection.

Dad didn't think Latin was necessary, so I didn't take it at any other schools, but I did have to learn it at St. Mary's. I wish I hadn't forgotten all of it. Dad said that I should take typing in high school, and that's the only thing I remembered him caring about. He wasn't difficult with me about grades, especially once he lost interest in me. It's just as well because I didn't get particularly good grades, just the same as the other kids, even though I had an IQ of 150, or so I was told.

I'm ashamed to say that as a boy in London I fell for a scam on the back of comic books. I was probably eleven years old or something, and it was targeted to boys like me, public school boys in the UK that liked reading about Hannibal. It hit me in my weak spot—I love Roman history. It said you could get 132 Roman soldiers for just $1.99, which was probably more than my week's allowance.

When they arrived in the mail they were just cheap, flat stamp soldiers. I wasn't that disappointed, I just thought I should have known at my age that of course it was too good to be true. What did I expect for that money? I didn't fall for Sea-Monkeys though (shrimp sold as novelty aquarium pets); I knew there was something wrong there.

Another comic book scam in the late 1960s was something that could see through walls, and there was also an ad with a boy with glasses and he could see through a girl's dress. A lot of boys fell for that, although I certainly didn't. Only the Roman soldiers.

I remember going to parties with my parents in London and usually the people hosting had kids. Mother always dressed me in cute outfits. I remember falling asleep at parties on occasion and my parents taking me home later. When Mother and Dad entertained I'd sit around and watch TV in their bedroom and they'd forget about me, so I'd stay up a good deal later than I would have ordinarily. It was a huge bedroom and they used it as both a bedroom and a den. Our flat was in what was once a big Victorian home. That's how I saw "Bewitched" and "Get Smart" for the first time, in black and white. It came on past my bedtime so ordinarily I missed it. I thought "Get Smart" was a real spy show and took it seriously at first. I wasn't very sophisticated at ten. "The Three Stooges" was funny but anything more subtle than that was lost on me.

At Mother and Dad's big parties our au pair did maid duties. Sometimes you have to have big parties like that, and Dad probably invited people from NATO. They were busy making a good impression. Dad had a food and drink book and he probably made drinks with it.

We went to St. Marks Church in London. Dad was friends with the vicar. Reverend Michael Dean was his name. Mother was friends with his wife, too. Anthony was their son, and we got our long pants together at St Mary's School. We were very involved in that church.

Christmas in London was a special time in those days. I remember 1966, and we had just one channel or maybe two, and color TV didn't come until after I left. Everybody was talking about it but it wasn't available until probably 1969. I recall that holiday morning and the special programming. British TV wasn't like in the US, where Saturday morning kids watch cartoons. That just wasn't done there. Nothing was on television during the day and programming didn't start until late in the afternoon. On that particular holiday they started off with a couple of "Laurel and Hardy" episodes, the one when they were singing at the end, and then they had an excellent movie called, *The Pickwick Papers*, a 1952 British film with Joyce Grenfell in it. For years I wanted to see it again and when I finally saw it on YouTube, and it was as good as I remembered.

In 1967 Mother took a drawing class alongside Lady Alec Guinness and some other ladies. She was an artist of some sort. Mother probably had many friends in that class but of course she mainly mentioned the famous person. It was a relatively small class and the man who taught it was a good artist. Mother took me along once for some reason, maybe before Francois the au pair was there. I've forgotten the artist's name, but he was one of those gentlemen who was really an artist, likely someone who'd studied at an art college in Europe. He'd ended up in London as a refugee so perhaps he learned at a college occupied by the Nazi regime.

Dad used to read a lot of paperbacks then. *The Executioner* was a series of spy stories in cheap paperbacks, and he also read history books. There was one he was reading about Nazi spies, and it had something with swastikas on the cover. I'd borrow his books to look at the covers. Sometimes I'd struggle to read them at age eleven or twelve. I remember Mother telling me I couldn't take the book with swastikas to art class because it would offend the art teacher. That made me think he was a refugee. Mother painted a jester in that class. The teacher guided her hand and did most of it.

Mother had a BBC book on how to paint and draw. The books were scarcely used. She did take care of things but if I was using a book to learn to draw, like the old catalogues, I really used them to copy, and so you would tell it had been used. Since Mother's is practically new (not a mint, but a B if it were a comic book), I know she didn't open it.

I remember bothering our au pair Francois on Saturdays to see if she'd take me to a movie. We'd look at the paper to see what was playing. I'd ask her to see a film and she'd have to tell me I couldn't because I was too young. They were strict in those days about letting young people in. In 1967 I couldn't get into *Dracula* or *Frankenstein*, old English Hammer movies now on TV; but back then even with an adult you couldn't get in. You had to be a teenager. We got turned away from *Cleopatra*, and the woman just said, "You can't go in with him, Love."

Back then families would go to movies on Friday nights, and go to dinner maybe and then a film. I remember Mother and Dad went to see *Bonnie and Clyde* but I certainly couldn't. They did take me to see *Thunderball* and *You Only Live Twice, James Bond,* and *Mary Poppins,* and Mother and Dad took me to see *Empress File* with Michael Kane at the Odeon Theater. Dad liked the movie *The Jokers*. It was a movie that came out when we were in London, and it had Oliver Reed in it. It is about two brothers who decide to steal the crown jewels.

Not long ago a friend from fifty years ago got in touch. We got long pants together at school in London, and he looked me up after all that time. I didn't call him back because I just didn't know what to say to him.

Mother was happiest in London and on the Riviera. She was out so much I never saw her. By the time we got to Brussels, Dad travelled a lot with NATO and she had no social life, and that was the first time I heard them really fight.

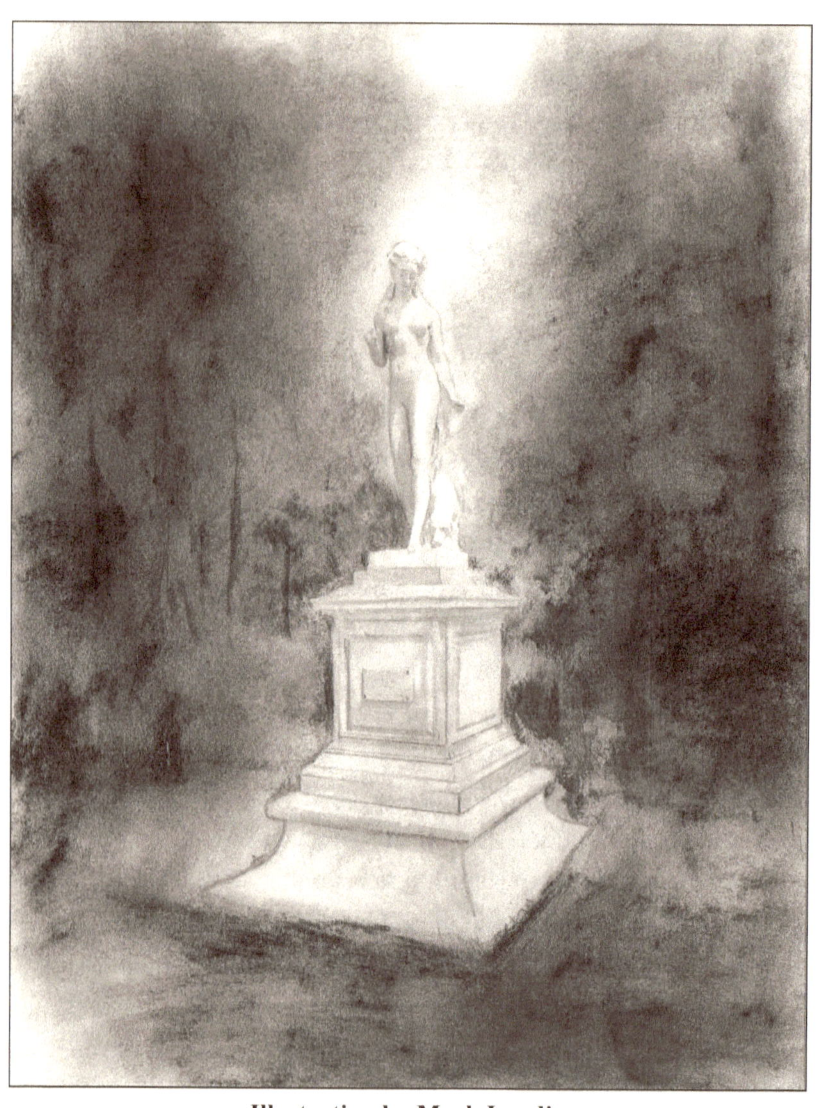

Illustration by Mark Landis

<u>4</u>

BRUSSELS

French President Charles de Gaulle had a row with the United States that resulted in Dad being transferred to Belgium. I still have Dad's "General Orders" letter, telling him about the "relocation of the Office of the Assistant United States Member of the Allied Radio Frequency Agency," dated August 1, 1967. It stated the Agency would be "disestablished at London, England" and "established in Brussels, Belgium." The "missions and functions … will remain the same."

We left London and went to Paris for a month before moving to Brussels in 1967. I have one very pleasant memory of when we were in Paris that has stayed with me. I remember it was summer, hot but not oppressive. We were staying at the Hotel Du Nord, in one of those hotel rooms with those big double windows they have in France, with a little handle on them, the kind that open up like doors to a faux balcony. Mother and Dad opened those windows and it was nice. Dad went across the street to the little stores and bought a lot of things to eat that didn't need to be cooked. He made a couple trips and I went with him. What was fun about it, was we kind of had a picnic in the room by the window, only it was better than an ordinary old picnic with ants.

What I enjoyed most about it all was all the nice packages; they had interesting advertising. There were nice boxes and tins for biscuits and crackers and I enjoyed looking at all of them, because they were things not really familiar to me. I was used to UK and American stuff. This was the 1960s, and I'm sure there are stores you can go to now to get imported things, but not back then. I liked looking at the wrappings. We had a real nice time in that hotel room with the windows open.

Mother and Dad were happy then.

Once we got to Brussels things changed. Mother and I were alone in the hotel room there. Mother didn't have as many friends, and we had trouble finding an apartment when we got there so we spent at least six to seven weeks in that hotel. Sometimes I want to say it was three months or so, but I doubt it was actually that long, because everything feels like a long time as a kid. The Hotel Metropol was a huge old hotel. Mother got upset if I listened to anything other than classical music, and she made me read certain things. There was no TV in the room, only out in the main area, but everything was in French and Flemish anyhow and no use to me.

There was a huge square with a theater across the street where they showed American movies. I remember there was a huge gaudy marquee for *The St. Valentine's Day Massacre,* which I wanted to see but they wouldn't let me in because I was too young. But other than seeing movies, the rest of the time Mother and I were alone in our hotel room. That was the period of our lives when we spent the most time together, except for when I moved in with her after the hurricane, when I was an adult.

One day she said, "I'm going to teach you to play bridge." We learned and it went on and on. "Well, we are having some fun," she'd say. Bridge was the main game we played because she wouldn't play games like gin because it wasn't sophisticated. Mother and I were closest when we were in that hotel room in Brussels.

Eventually they found us an apartment. At the neighbourhood theater I'd watch bad westerns in French with Flemish subtitles. We lived there for a while. Outside our place in Brussels there was a nice Victorian statue, some sort of nymph. One day boys were throwing dirty clods at it, and I thought it was so mean. I looked at her and thought, *I'm sorry.* We were there for nearly a year. I remember we came back to the US in the summer. I liked the movie *The Heart is a Lonely Hunter* because Mother and I saw it on the ship. It made a lasting impression on me.

I remember a fair with a shooting gallery in Belgium. The thing was probably rigged. I was the best shot. When I was young I seldom elicited much praise of any kind from my friends but that time I did. I guess Americans are better at shooting than most people. I remember Dad got me a bag of donut holes—probably better than the stuff you get here. It had lots of powdered sugar on it. I believe Dad was proud of me that day.

The thing is, I maybe didn't make Dad very proud, but I also didn't have many embarrassing things happen to me as a boy. It likely wouldn't have mattered to me until later anyhow. One thing I remember is that a lot of the books I tried to struggle through were old, and so the use of language tended to be archaic. People still misunderstand me sometimes. I'll just use a word in the way it was meant to be understood a long time ago, not in the way it is used now.

In school in Belgium I read something out loud and said something along the lines of, "it was thereby hoped that Sir John Fairbanks served to the court some intercourse between nations…" I used the word 'intercourse' in the way it was meant to be used. I remember the teacher was laughing and laughing and said, "You bad boy," not in a mean way, but in a joking way, and I had no idea what it was she was laughing about.

I remember another teacher in the hall laughing at me too. It was a couple of years before I realized what was going on. I thought, *you have a lot of nerve laughing at me about that.* How was I supposed to know? I've now gone through all kinds of changes in society and now gone on to see word use change a lot. When I was older at the Menninger Clinic, I knew one or two people who were gay, but I still used the word the way it was originally used, and I'd say things like "I'm happy and gay." I was nineteen or something when I realized "gay" didn't mean that anymore.

In Brussels one woman wanted to make friends with Mother but her husband was a sergeant and Mother was always going on about how much better their apartment was. Dad was a lieutenant commander. They had two nice daughters, but Mother just didn't want anything to do with them.

The first argument I overheard was in Brussels. Mother just wasn't happy after leaving London because she didn't have as many friends and she wanted to go to Paris but they couldn't. Dad was gone quite a bit and Mother was lonely. I remember it was Christmas in Belgium in 1967 or 1968 when I first noticed Mother and Dad fighting. It was pretty depressing because even though it was Christmas, there was no holiday programming on to distract me. The fight was about money, which is very common. The only time I ever saw Mother cry was when she was fighting with Dad. She'd resort to tears to be dramatic, just like in a situation comedy.

They fought over money because they always lived slightly beyond their means. When Grandfather died they were left some money and they were kind of irresponsible. Irresponsible is maybe a bad word … I would say they were extravagant, so they spent it all. Dad spent money on expensive cars and Mother spent money on clothes and jewellery. They were both extravagant. I remember going with Dad to get a new grey Mercedes at the factory in Germany in 1964. It was still with him in 1972. I was awfully young, probably about seven or eight. In 1967 or 1968 Dad bought a new red Spitfire. It went over with us on the ship.

We went to London again before we went home to the U.S. from Brussels. Mother wanted to see her friends again and Dad had something to do with NATO and I think that's when Dad bought the Spitfire and it came home with us. Mother bought an extravagant red Cadillac the year before she died. I do remember we were briefly in Long Beach for a while before we went someplace else, but we were not there long, and I think Dad drove Mother and I all the way across the country in the Triumph Spitfire.

All the cars had cigarette lighters. Dad smoked and Mother took it up because she thought it was fashionable but quit just like that; she had no difficulty quitting because it meant nothing to her. When I was real, real little, somehow I managed to get the lighter out and I tried doing what I saw them doing and I burned my wrist real badly. It was the first very painful accident I remember.

I attended an Anglo-American School from late 1967 to June or July 1968. Outside of school there was nothing for me to do but copy art books, which is how I got good at copying, or struggle with reading books. We didn't have a TV in Brussels. All military families my age will have this resonate: the currents were different in Europe and Dad just didn't want to bother with a big bulky transformer. So, I spent a lot of time at the English library. Mother would take me there, and sometimes she'd go shopping and then come back and get me. It didn't have a big sign and was just a couple of rooms on one floor of one of those big old ornate buildings in downtown Brussels.

Most of the books there were pretty old; the latest thing was probably written in 1930 or something. I don't know if they had a young people's section. I guess I got attracted by the bindings, but I ended up struggling through difficult old books, some Victorian, and my parents expected me to persevere through them. It was good for me struggling through those books. That's why I speak so well, the influence of those books. I had an idea it would be an accomplishment if I got through Ludwig's poetry. It was pretty intimidating to someone just twelve or thirteen.

I loved *Life with Father.* I could read that book over and over, but I liked the movie better. It was written in the 1920s and serialized in *The New Yorker*. It's about growing up, but the father is the one you remember from the book. There were things about the father in that book—mainly political and social opinions—that were so much like Dad. That's probably why the book is so remembered even now; it probably described so many fathers … the way a dad ought to be. When I was in Belgium I could spend a whole day looking at a good book. You can read to escape the unpleasantness of life. Libraries have always been a good friend to me.

I had my thirteenth birthday in Brussels. It was just me, Mother and Dad. It wouldn't have occurred to me at the time to invite a lot of kids and get a lot of presents. We went to a good French restaurant. I had crepe suzette with orange peels and things like powdered sugar, not ones like you'd get at International House of Pancakes. I remember them well. We didn't have a TV so after dinner we went to see a movie, a famous musical from Broadway that they'd made it into a good movie, called *A Funny Thing Happened on the Way to the Forum*. Then Mother and Dad drove me home where I got some presents.

Sometimes they were trying to think of things that would be presents any teenager would want, but a lot of times they went wrong. They gave me a transistor radio, with a little ear plug I think, a fashionable thing for teens at that time. It was nice but I would have rather had something else. It was a good present, a quality present. But at that time I was collecting stamps so maybe I would have rather had that. Mother ended up using it and would play classical music on my transistor. She would go into my bedroom and put it on for me because I wasn't much using it. I tried going to sleep to it but that was about it.

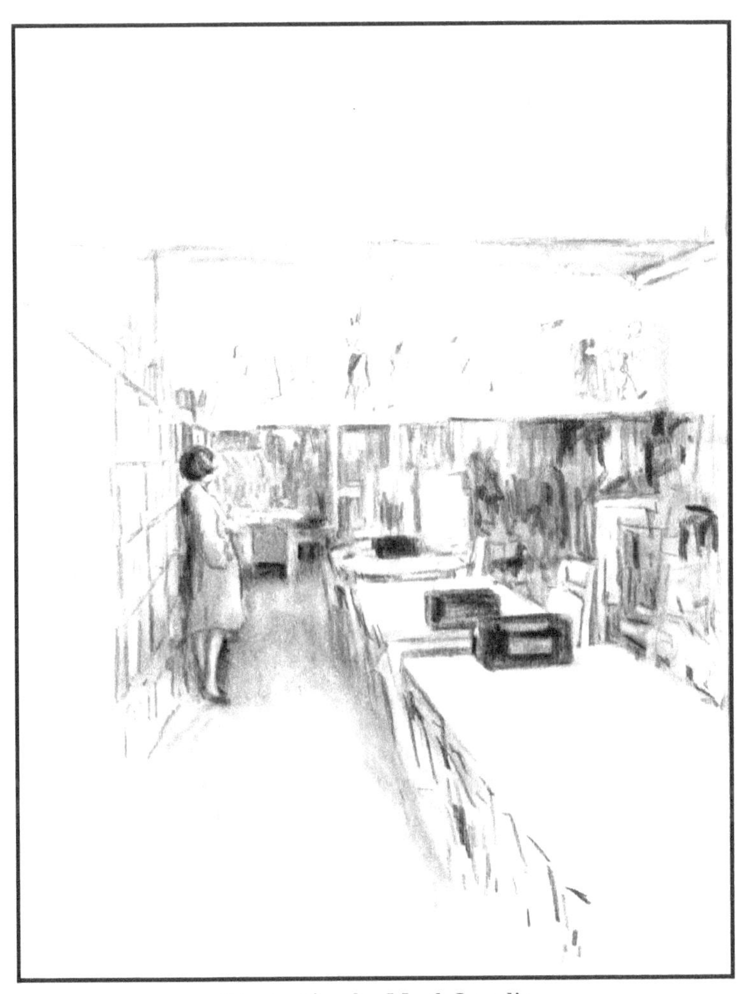

Illustration by Mark Landis

<u>**5**</u>

WASHINGTON, D.C.

When we came back to the US we lived in Washington—in Chevy Chase, Maryland, actually—in 1968, and lived there in 1969, and part of 1970. In my new bedroom I had my father's furniture from when he was a boy, and a Currier and Ives picture of a clipper ship on the wall that had belonged to the family. I did not have the picture of Chinese babies burning in flames yet. We lived in a big apartment building in Chevy Chase, called the Willoughby, apartment 1417, which later became condominiums in the 1980s but still looks the same.

I attended St. Andrew's Church in Maryland. There is a good private school for boys attached to the cathedral, and Mother and Dad wanted me to go there but it was too expensive. I remember them talking about it. Dad had cousins nearby named the Harleys and they were pretty wealthy and their son went there, so of course Mother would want me there because it was prestigious. I got to go to St Mary's in London because the government paid—a benefit of NATO—but this time they wouldn't pay for it. Dad was friends with Father Dean at St. Andrews. I still have my old Sunday school book from then.

I attended Westland Middle School but back then it was Westland Junior High. I'm a "notable boy" there on their website, like I am at St. Mary's Town and Country School in London. I eventually fit in there and made friends and got along quite nicely. They had me do a mural in the library which I painted to get out of gym class. That library reminds me of one in an episode of "Room 222;" it looked very much like that one. My mural showed the evolution of man right up to the moon landing. I was a hero for doing it and they gave me a special award at an assembly and everyone cheered. They took it down to renovate even though it commemorated the moonwalk the year it happened, like the monks cutting the bottom off The Last Supper for a kitchen … it seemed like a pressing need at the time. It's not as bad as that example, but it's bad enough. There are lots of examples of what people have done to art that was crazy. Things are always obvious in retrospect. A recent principal wrote me to say she was sorry the mural was gone, even though she wasn't on staff there back in the 1990s.

I remember the ad in the back of magazines where you copy a picture of a little turtle and you can become a children's illustrator. I think I did it in class. It was actually a reputable school. I looked on the Internet recently. I drew the picture and sent it in and they wrote back and said the usual, that I had talent, and I showed it to Mother and she showed it to Dad who said it was a con. Things are seldom what they seem. It didn't matter because I got to draw the picture and learn that way. You'd be impressed by the graduates of that school. Whereas with the Famous Author School, one that did turn out to be a complete fraud, you would read the letter and think it was your calling … but everybody was accepted. "Twilight Zone" creator   Rod Serling used to pitch it himself.

I remember in school thinking I wish I could do the cover on those pulp paperbacks. My modest ambitions were best for me, just becoming a humble commercial artist. They had fantastic covers—you basically bought the cover—but inside the stories had almost nothing to do with the picture on the front. That's how it was in the golden ages of pulps and paperbacks before TV. The cover sold the book but by then they weren't doing those things anymore.

I bought comic books when I was young, but they were badly drawn. They certainly aren't now—they are masterpieces—and people in the industry go to school a long time and students really train to illustrate them and they are talented people. The first Superman, the first appearance of Batman—that stuff is worth a lot of money. Mother threw my comic books away because they were trashy, violent, and poorly drawn. I wasn't upset when she did it. That's why the comic books that remain are so valuable. Mothers threw them out. No mother ever threw away a Bible. You can buy a two-hundred-year-old Bible for $200, whereas comic books from the 1950s are worth so much money. I remember getting the American Heritage Junior Library books as presents or out of the library. They were meant for kids. I have one on American trappers and mountain men. They were big books and had lots of pictures in them. I kept ones I was real fond of and it was good of Mother not to give them away.

The ones I had when I was younger are in storage because I can't keep everything in the apartment, but I'll dig them out eventually. I did find one at the Salvation Army. They bring back a lot of good memories. I grew up with them and that's how I learned about history. They had a good one on the French/Indian war, the Spanish/American war, a big deluxe one for the Civil War.

I never dated as a teenager. If I did have crushes it would only have been someone on TV. You know that Norman Rockwell cover? Well as a teenager that would sort of be me. When I was in high school I was kind of different from most of the other young people. As an example, I can remember standing in line behind two high school girls and I was listening to them, and one girl said, "Oh I went to see *Love Story* again … it was my fifth time and I cried and cried."

I never saw it but it seemed like a sickening film. My favorite episode of "The Outer Limits" with Donald Pleasence was called, "The Man with the Power." The character was a little college professor, a shy man and he was kind of a failure who taught at a low-rated college, but he came up with this invention, some kind of chip between his eyes. That's why it was called The Man with the Power. He'd never get mad or anything, because if he was irritated a cloud would form over the people who bothered him and it would obliterate them to dust. I remember thinking the teenage girls were such stupid, useless creatures, quite juvenile, even if I was a teenager too, and if I was the man with the power they'd be off the planet. I couldn't help thinking it was really too bad that I couldn't be like him.

I could draw well as a teenager. One girl was the queen of something, Miss Mississippi or something, and she just kind of ordered me to draw her. Many people did that.

I made a friend named Phillip at Westland Junior High and we had cotillion class together. It was every Friday night during the season, and there were quite a few of them. We learned how to dance and learned social skills. I went to Phillip's birthday party. I believe he ended up going to St. Andrew's school after ninth grade.

In 1969 there was a cotillion at school. The boys would ask the girls to dance and you'd get them a refreshment. There were dances when the girls would ask the boys to dance. I was an awkward boy with poor self-esteem when I was thirteen, really the lowest possible self-esteem. There are unattractive little boys with low self-esteem and socially unpopular, but there are also little girls like that too, who were referred to as wallflowers at the time.

There was one blonde girl I remember; the last week of classes she had a cast on her arm. Even at the time I noticed her clothes were very out of fashion, made from simple patterns from 1968 or 1969, and it was 1972. Any girls that might have been mean to her are all old now and are probably sorry, assuming they remember anyway.

I had a silent understanding with that girl. I scarcely remember talking to her, but we had a silent agreement: if I asked her to dance, she would. I made sure she never suffered any social humiliation, and she did the same for me. We never let each other down. At the dance I'd ask her if she wanted refreshments but that's all we ever said. You never forget how to fox trot, although I forgot how to tango. I'll always remember that girl and how we protected each other from social disaster.

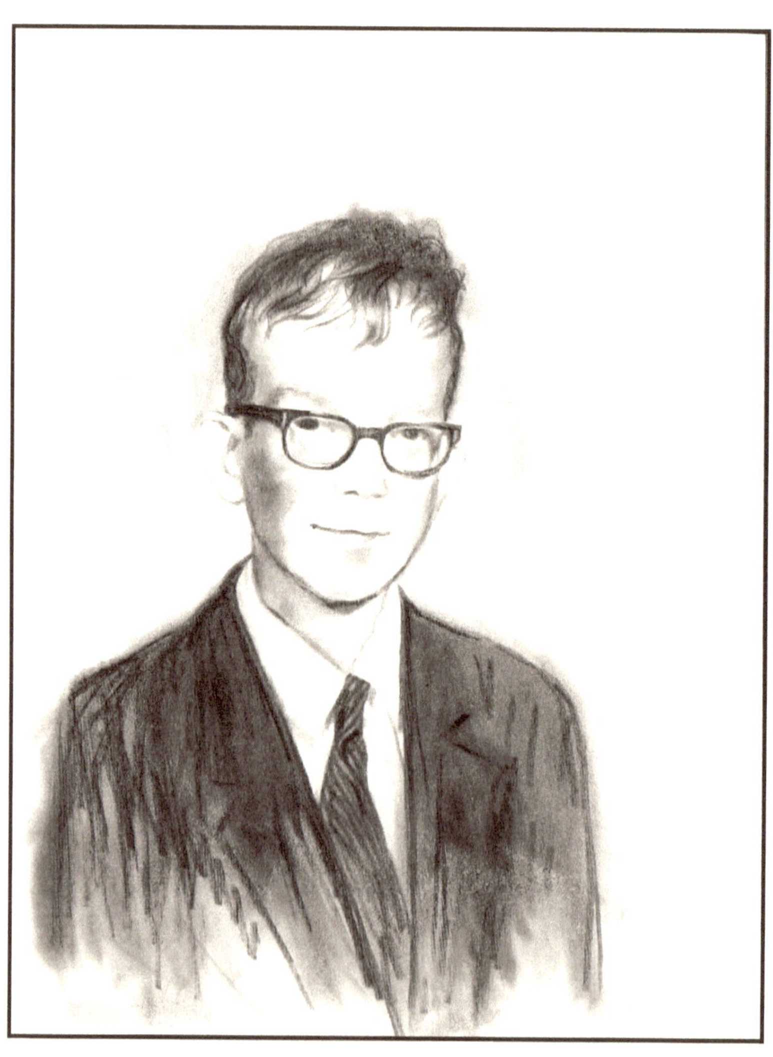

Me at age 17. Illustration by Mark Landis

<u>6</u>

HIGH SCHOOL DAYS

It wouldn't have occurred to me to ask to not move or to stay somewhere, because moving is just what we did. Oscar Wilde wondered if art imitates life more than life imitates art. I think life imitates TV more than TV imitates life. TV plagiarizes life and life imitates TV—that's how I like to put it. We've all seen episodes where a family is going to move and the kids don't want to, and more often than not they get used to the idea of moving. As far as my family goes it would not have occurred to me to object or complain. I remember I just accepted things. In a way it was kind of exciting.

When we moved Mother and Dad bought a house in Clinton Mississippi, which is a suburb of Jackson. It was a new suburban house, a nice house. We moved there because Dad was passed over for promotion—that was a complete disaster—so he had to retire. I was a big disappointment in Washington anyway.

Mother didn't have many friends in Brussels or in Washington, and she decided she wanted to be near her family. It wasn't that kind of marriage where Mother imposed what she wanted; it was fairly equal when they made decisions. They did argue sometimes. I remember in Brussels them arguing about money and in Washington the arguments were about money as well. When I think of Dad he's still intimidating and older, but he was only in his forties at that time … I could have been his father now. Anyhow, Mother eventually talked Dad into moving to Mississippi.

In Jackson we had a newish suburban house like on the "Brady Bunch" or the "Smith Family." Really it was a house like on any 1970s situation comedy. It was difficult to tell if Mother was happy. She was relatively happy in Washington with friends. She was somewhat happier than Brussels, but she was never as happy as she was in London and

France. It sounds odd to say, but London and France were where she felt most at home.

After leaving Chevy Chase I didn't adjust to Jackson right away. It's a hard age to make a drastic move. I started at Clinton High School. That was indeed a culture shock. I don't have any happy memories from there. Of course, I was nervous about the first day of school. No one wants to be the new boy at school unless you're exceptionally talented or good looking, where success is guaranteed. If you're sort of ordinary you don't look forward to it.

The students at Clinton High were surprised about me being there. They were surprised Dad would want to retire in Mississippi. They had a low opinion of Jackson, although it wasn't that bad of a place; it wasn't like *The Heart Is a Lonely Hunter*. There was prejudice but it wasn't like in the movies. I had two Black teachers and lots of Black students which I hadn't experienced before. There is still prejudice today. People stay the same over time and just the clothes change. I remember when I went back to the school in 1990, it was just the same. There were still those desks with the little arm rests, like nothing has changed. I remember thinking to myself, *Gee, it's just like last time.*

Moving to Mississippi was a big change, and I did not like it as it seemed like an awfully backwards place. I missed the TV channels in Washington. It wasn't exactly like the books you read where somebody moves to a coffee plantation, like *The Flame Trees of Thika*, not that drastic a change, but it was still a bit much. That was really when I stayed in my room a lot and didn't make any friends. I never really adjusted. Mother was good to me, but she was just the same as any other mother, and she banished me to the garage to paint because I got paint on the rug. There was nothing to do out there so I listened to opera.

I can't remember if I walked to school each day or if Mother drove me. The school library had an encyclopaedia of the history of art. It was a big set—like twelve volumes or something like that—one set for artists of different centuries. They were reference books. In the back they had a lot of drawings and paintings of the great artists of that period. I'd take them home. Mother and Dad got me a TV set when I was sixteen, so I'd sit and watch TV and copy pictures out of the book. That's how I developed my drawing. I do remember bringing them back at the end of the term. I don't remember who, maybe it was a librarian or teacher, but somebody said I wasn't supposed to have taken them home, but they were nice and said it didn't matter. I also went to the public library in Clinton and Jackson, and the Mississippi College library. As I've said before, libraries have always been very important to me.

I have no complaints about any of my teachers. There was no one special but no one I want to complain about either. Some people have memories of teachers that kept them from succeeding or had it in for them. I don't have any fond memories or bad memories. There are few pictures of me as a teenager because in those days you took pictures of your kids when they were children, and you often stopped taking photos as they got older. In high school I was in class with a girl named Maria Shriver (not Arnold's wife, but the one who went to Mississippi College). I can't tell you anything about her because we weren't in the same set. I can't remember her at all.

I'd adjusted moving to every place through the years but not this time. Mother and Dad were fighting. In Dad's New Testament Bible (everyone got them when you graduated, and his has his name in it so it was a present) I'd found "Ambition's Prayer" taped into his bible, which he'd cut from the newspaper. The first time I saw it, it really got to me. I know why he'd put that there. As a young ensign he was full of ambition. He got passed over as lieutenant commander and had to retire and got cancer and died. Dad was no doubt expecting a better career. That's why I ended up reading so many history books, so Dad would be pleased with me. But Dad never made history. He did okay climbing the ladder the way you'd expect.

When I was going through whatever I was going through the first year I moved from Washington, Dad got mad at me. I got sick physically around 1970. That was when I started reading a lot because we didn't have many TV channels. I just sort of lay around, not catatonic, but I didn't move much. I kept throwing up and they didn't know what was wrong. I had a lot of problems. At first, I wouldn't come out of the room and stopped speaking to people, and I kind of behaved like a young Helen Keller, at times. I stopped eating and lost an awful lot of weight and Mother was worried. I looked like one of those little boys who got out of a concentration camp in the war.

Mother had me seeing regular medical doctors who made house calls. They thought it was something to do with growing up, the maturing process of the body; but they didn't really know, and one thing led to another, and if they couldn't find a medical reason they decided it had to be psychosomatic. I remember Dad getting frustrated. The doctor told Dad it was psychosomatic. I remember Dad coming in mad and telling me he wanted me to get well and he took away the portable TV set. He was just mad. I got it back a couple days later.

I can understand he was just frustrated—it's something dads do—and it's no reflection on him. Dad was a fine gentleman. I saw someone act like that on a TV show, in a number of shows actually, where parents will get frustrated with somebody. I don't blame him and anyway it was just the doctor's fault for telling Dad I was psychosomatic.

Mother used to take me to the pharmacy for a special milkshake each day as part of a weight-gain program. It was a pleasant memory because they had young people working there and I enjoyed interacting with them. I stabilized for a little bit and went back to school for the next semester of the tenth grade. But that summer was disastrous because Dad got sick and was diagnosed with cancer. It was one thing after another, and being a teenager made it difficult.

Dad died of cancer when he was just 46 or 47. He got a realtor's licence and tried to get into real estate, but he got cancer and died before he even got started in his new career. Dad was real brave when he was dying. He just sort of carried on the way he always did and never looked upset, at least not around me, and I doubt if he did around Mother either because it was a pretty small house. Mother tried to keep herself from looking upset but it was obvious that she was, and just like how Archie Bunker said "stifle," I got the impression Mother was stifling it. Dad read as long as he could until his eyes swelled up the week before he died. He was in the hospital a lot, but I'd go visit him there.

He was at home when he died. I was in the house. He didn't have a hospital bed or anything, but there was a formal sitting room no one went into and he watched TV in there. Dad went into the TV room and he expired on the couch. They had given him a few more months to live, so when it happened, it was somewhat sooner than expected. TV dads have a heart to heart with sons and make big apologies to them, but it wasn't like that at all with him. It was just business as usual. When he died there was absolutely nothing sentimental about it and he didn't want any last talks with me.

I admire him very much for how brave he was. I do remember my dad collected himself and wrote letters of instructions, to my great-aunt and to Mother. The letters were probably nothing emotional. When I think about him now, he still seems older. They had a small service for Dad just before I went to the hospital. The only funeral I have ever been to was Dad's. The coffin was sealed. I believe he had a military service and there was a salute from the sailors present.

I started going down the first of the eleventh grade and I ended up at a hospital in Jackson, the University of Mississippi Medical Center (UMMC). I was in a ward for a day, and they made me drink some awful drink for the weight loss, and I remember the nurse and doctor telling me I had to drink it or they'd feed me through an intravenous tube. That's how I ended up at the hospital initially. They threw around the usual explanations, and thought it was all because of our relocation to Mississippi. It's true, I didn't like the move so much, mainly because I missed Washington because they had a big art museum and lots of TV channels. But I felt I had adjusted.

I ended up in the psychiatric unit of the hospital. They tossed around those mental health terms, like "bi-polar" and "wild mood swings," but that could be any teenager. It doesn't mean they are bi-polar. But it wasn't the dark ages of mental health; it was like an episode of "Marcus Welby MD." If you had to go to a hospital for behavior problems, it was better back then than it is today, when it is just medication and complete indifference.

I've made friends with doctors now who work there and they say it's much the same today. Very few people were treated there long term because it is a medical hospital. If you were under eighteen, they would keep you there as long as they could because there were no state hospitals for children with mental or behavior problems. Once you were eighteen you could be sent to the state mental health facility. I did start getting a bit better but I don't give the hospital any credit for it. I personally think I got better because my body physically matured as I transitioned to adulthood.

But that was when I started misbehaving, probably because you can't help but to be influenced by the people you are around. If you are thrown in with a group of mental patients with behavior problems, you are going to act out a bit. That's when the Devil in me came out and I behaved worse than I did before I entered the hospital. I was in the company of retarded people—yes, I know they call it an intellectual disability now, but then they called it being retarded—and since I was in that club I can use that word without the uncomfortable sting of being politically incorrect. When it comes to psychiatry and psychology, you are who they say you are.

I was in the hospital for nine months. Sometimes they kept me segregated from the other patients. They brought my meals to me on a tray and I had no privileges. I deserved it for my bad behavior in the ward. They called my treatment behavior modification. I was very uncommunicative at the time and very unpredictable. Think in terms of a young Helen Keller rather than someone doing violent or doing mean things. I just did not talk much or respond to questions.

One of the things that got me in trouble was my skill as a pickpocket. I knew I wouldn't be particularly punished. The doctor I liked the most was Dr. Johnson. I once took his wallet and didn't give it back right away. I only got away with it once and then he was on his guard, and I didn't do it again. It just became a routine on our walks for him to be careful about me getting too close to his wallet. He was a very good and excellent doctor. He suggested I go to a trade school that taught drawing and was affiliated with Hallmark, but his recommendation did not get approved by Mother. Looking back, she should have heeded him. I got caught a couple times trying to pickpocket from other doctors. I knew nothing would happen, other than lose privileges. I was bad. But I was interested in magic and sleight of hand. There was one aide who I was mad at, so I picked his pocket and threw his wallet into the lake.

It all sounds bad now, but it wasn't that terrible. At some point, Mother sent in a radio and tons of books. It was good for me in a way because I became very well read. One good sentence speaks pages. There is no frigate that can take you away like a book, which is safer and cheaper. The doctors were friendly and nice enough, but didn't have time to build a relationship with me. I remember one time a doctor came to see me and said, "This is not a punishment because you stay in your room all the time anyway." I think he was just trying to make himself feel better.

Recently, I took the trouble to read my diagnostic papers from that time period again. I don't agree with a lot of it. I do like the schizophrenia diagnosis because I'm used to it. They didn't have all the complicated diagnoses they do nowadays. Schizophrenia was nice and simple.

It was while I was being treated at UMMC that I got my *A Pictorial History of the Silent Screen,* which I'd seen in a bookstore, and why I got interested in making a film on the life of St Laurence. Mother gave it to me. I would spend hours and hours looking at this book of old stills, wondering what those movies and stories were about. I'd wonder about the films. Some things I recognized—like the ones based on Shakespeare's plays. Later on, I'd go to the library and stand in front of the stacks of magazines and read a journal about motion pictures that went back to 1900. It was wonderful. You could read about films to go with the still pictures I knew. The best thing about YouTube is after all those years I can finally see many of those of the films.

I read on Quora that things were worse in mental hospitals in the 1970s than they are today. Mental health treatment was said to be inferior in most places to what it is today. That wasn't true in my experience. There was more individual attention and people were interested in you. I mean, there were some things that were bad, but I have no complaints. Mostly they were good to me, even being separated from the others was good for me because I read a lot. I knew people who had electroshock therapy. I don't know if it did them any good or not, but they always seem to feel it was an interesting conversation if they mentioned it.

They arranged for me later in my stay to keep up some with schoolwork. I had taken my SATs before the hospital and they were average. In those days I don't think people studied for them. I did a term paper in the hospital because they did want me to graduate. I might have gone for a test too, but I can't remember it. It was 1973.

An aide took me in a cab to hand in the term paper and have the graduation picture done. All of the tuxedos are false fronts that slipped on very easily. Apparently, the girls had something similar as they all look the same. I don't like the picture. I looked awful. I left the hospital for the photo, so my hair wasn't great and I had a shabby appearance. I didn't shave for the photo, because obviously they wouldn't give you razors in the hospital. I didn't see anyone I knew, and no one asked where I'd been.

My graduation photo was terrible, so my favorite photo of me is when I was sixteen. I'm wearing a thin tie and a nice suit. It looks dignified.

Someone who knew me in high school recently got in touch with my friend Sam. We'd gone to school together and he still had his yearbook and sent a picture. I don't remember him. I look at the page and I don't remember any of them. I had no particular friends there and can remember very few names. None of the teenagers in the yearbook are familiar and we all look very extremely unpromising and very unlikely to succeed although, I would certainly wish them well. The artist Wyatt Waters went to the school and is well known in Mississippi; he decorated the walls of the restaurant The Purple Parrot. I do not remember him at all.

In high school I do remember one girl in my algebra class. She must not have had a family with much money. Her clothes were homemade from sewing patterns, but she always looked real nice. We were in class together and two girls, both from upper rungs of the social ladder, would say mean things to her. She had a nice roundish face. Looking at the girls in the yearbook reminded me of that. One girl always tried out for cheerleading, but she was so terrible the other kids refrained from talking to her. High school students aren't necessarily all mean.

I didn't get my diploma the day of the photograph. One of Mother's friends decided that although the doctors kind of wanted to commit me and send me to a locked state facility, I should be sent to the Menninger Clinic instead. So, after several months I left Mississippi and headed to the Menninger Clinic. My diploma was mailed to me there.

[Publisher's Note: We tried to verify the information about Mark Landis' stay at UMMC, but the Health Insurance Portability and Accountability Act (HIPAA) prohibits the release of such information about patients. A hospital spokesperson said there is not a residency program in the psychiatry department today and there is no evidence one existed 50 years ago in the early 1970s. However, there is evidence Landis was treated by a UMMC psychiatrist and he may have been held there for nine months as a special case.]

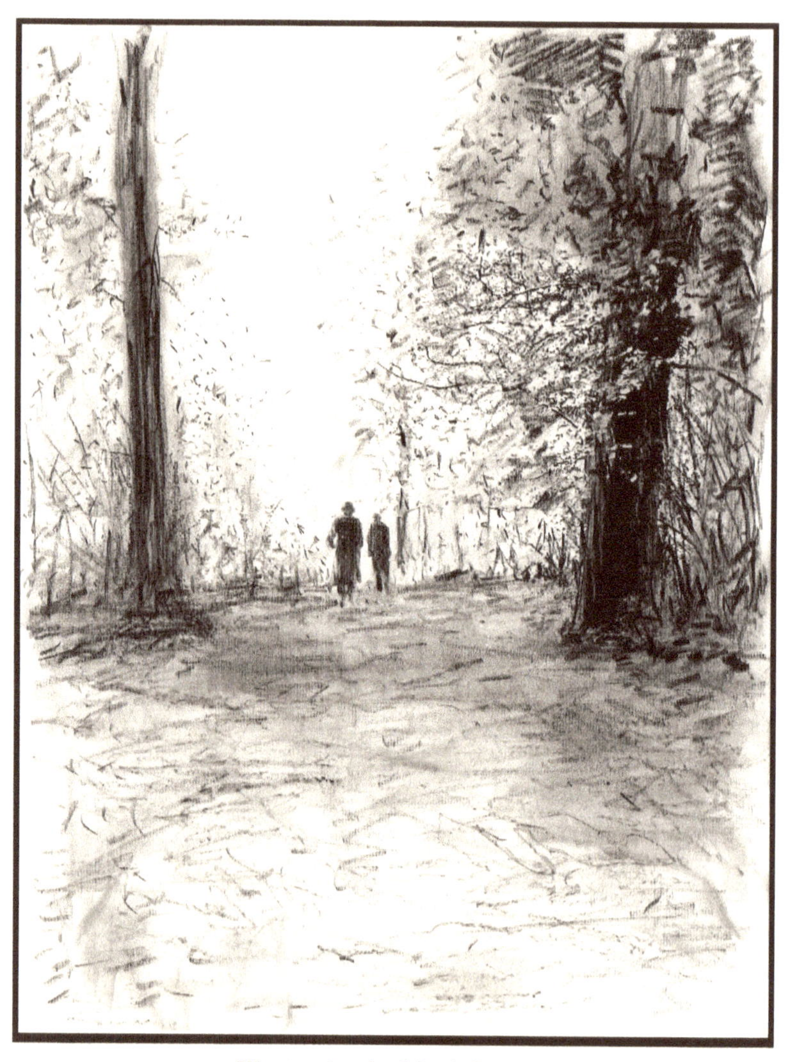

Illustration by Mark Landis

<u>7</u>

THE MENNINGER FOUNDATION

Mother's friend was a lady named Myra Hamilton Greene, somebody who was socially prominent, like in *Driving Miss Daisy*, that same social class, and what passed for high society in Jackson in those days. That's the sort of lady Mother tried to make friends with. She was from an old family from Jackson Missouri, and she had a big old house. She'd studied at the Art Students' League in the 1940s and was a noted artist. Her paintings are still in Jackson. She taught classes. This lady took an interest in me in high school when Mother showed her my artwork and she thought I was some kind of a prodigy.

When I was at the University of Mississippi Medical Center, Mrs. Greene told Mother I should be at the Menninger Clinic, which was an exclusive place to send me. It was also expensive, but Mother managed to get the government to pay for it because Dad was military. They stopped paying eventually. There was one other place they considered, a rival place that was recommended, but Mrs. Greene said they relied too much on behaviour modification. They still had to use some behaviour modification at Menninger, but it wasn't quite so much.

When I went to Menninger, mental institutions were sometimes snake pits, like in the movie *Bill*. The real Bill wasn't mentally retarded. He was the way he was because he was neglected in that snake pit. Everyone would be if they were left there. He was actually right on the average intelligence line. Sure, there are problems with mental institutions now and you get medications that might harm more than help, but they are much better nowadays.

The C. F. Menninger Memorial Hospital was located at 5800 S.W. 6th Avenue in Topeka, Kansas. It was considered a reputable place and consisted of an entire campus on over four hundred acres. The main building was a huge four-story building and made of red brick with a giant clock tower in its center and it was once a hospital before the Menninger Foundation bought it. Inside it was a lot like the movie *The Breakfast Club*. People who wouldn't be friends were thrown together and because we were teens they befriended me. I made friends on my ward. Our bedrooms weren't locked, only the main doors. For the most part rooms had two people. But they put me in a separate room, probably because when I first went in I had behavior problems.

One girl I wouldn't normally be friends with, who wouldn't talk to me ordinarily, was named Lucia. She was real fashionable, with long blonde hair all the way to her knees. I first met Lucia when she took interest in me, which was good of her. It was in the recreation room. Oliver Sacks would have called the recreation room the "spiritual death." It was like in that movie *Awakenings*. Lucia sat down in front of me and said, "Mark! Draw my picture!" Even after I left the art institute, later in life no one wanted me to sketch their portrait.

Lucia was there for the things teenagers do, getting into trouble. Their families try to avoid something worse and put them in a hospital for a while. One of the boys had done something gutsy, something really bad, but I didn't find out what it was. Lucia was just being a bad girl, shoplifting, experimenting with drugs and drinking. There were three young men, Ken, and Alan (who was real popular and had girlfriends), and John (who would sometimes give me his clothes). Lucia was Alan's girlfriend for a while. He had girlfriends on the other wards, too. Another boy, Roger, had had a disastrous trip through life, with lots of drugs, the real bad ones you'd take back then, like LSD. The young friends who took me up, they really included me, and all the credit should go to them for helping me out during that time.

I do believe the Menninger Clinic helped us. There were some young people who killed themselves, but they were older, between 25-30, so not in our circle. We knew them but didn't spend time with them. There was one boy, Tom. He was our age but he was completely unaware of his environment. It could be 5 degrees Fahrenheit—very cold—and he could be in a T-shirt or not have a shirt on at all and be completely unaware. He could probably have been burned and he wouldn't know. His leg was always moving. We would talk to him. We'd go into each other's room to say hello and talk so he'd come in sometimes, but then he'd just get up and go somewhere else.

We had the odd scandal, like pregnancies. I remember the young men smoking in their rooms, although when I was at the hospital before that the patients and aides were also smoking in their rooms. Things have changed.

I used to help the young men smuggle in liquor. We went out with an aide on age-appropriate outings. One had a fake drivers' licence and could buy liquor in town, and then they'd hide it on the grounds in a prearranged place. When you came back from outings you were searched if they thought you had a drug and alcohol problem. I never drank myself, so no one was ever suspicious of me and I was never searched. I worked my way up in privileges to being allowed to walk from the ward to the canteen. The canteen had a ping pong table and pool table, and you could buy milkshakes there.

That's when I would go pick up the liquor for the boys and smuggle it back in. Sometimes I'd feel bad about it. They never tried to get me to drink. They would want me to stay and talk with them, but I used to watch the TV—it was in the separate TV room—and on those occasions I'd be running back and forth between commercials and talking to them. One of the counsellors told me they were just being friends to use me, but now I know that's not true because they stayed friends with me and one looked me up later. Those were the days when it cost a lot to make a long-distance call. If you didn't have the money to make a call, you had to mail a letter. I didn't lose touch with people until the 1980s.

They were indeed good friends to me. I remember John, the Beverly Hills boy, once called connections of his family in Chicago, like an art dealer. I was just nineteen so there was no interest in me in terms of art, but he just gave me contacts in case I had general questions, like getting around in a big city. He just wanted me to have contacts in case I needed anything.

The teens at Menninger were all a year older than me. Some took classes at Washburn but didn't go to the school. I could have spent more time with them, but I was always watching TV in the commons room, even though I used to come out on commercial breaks and visit with them in their room but then run back. It was like being in politics if you wanted to watch something. You had to persuade people to vote for it. There weren't a lot of choices in those days so more than not I got to see the shows I wanted. They probably already had an inclination to watch it anyhow.

In my files from Menninger it said I didn't have any "age-appropriate interests." That means I wouldn't have been a character on a sitcom. I doubt if I could even fit in as a character on an old episode of "Degrassi Jr. High." Not having age-appropriate behavior was one of the things they wanted to deal with, other than my having really bad social skills.

I was a unique teenager, never bought a record and had no idea what was going on with pop music. I listened to classical. I liked a couple of Disney storybook records, but I was probably the only teen who never bought a record. Mother hated contemporary music and I learned to have contempt for it from her. I never bought a record album or anything like that because Mother didn't approve of it. She liked Debussy and Dad liked Big Band because it was of his time. I liked Rameau, a French composer, and "Dance of the Savage." He was my favorite for some years.

In 1953 there was a film called the *5000 Fingers of Dr. T*, about a little boy who was forced to take piano lessons. In the 1930s Dad had an experience like that, where my grandmother made him take lessons, and lots of little boys were forced by well-intentioned mothers. Mother wanted me to take piano lessons, but Dad was against it because he'd hated his teacher. I'm not musical but I listen to classical to improve myself. It wasn't until 1989 when I lived in a group home that I knew about pop music. The only thing anyone watched then was MTV. Every so often an aide would find a subtle way to watch one of her own shows, but generally it was too dangerous to watch anything else because if an aide said it was time to do something you couldn't watch the end and people would get upset. MTV or VH1 were easier to turn off. That's how I knew hit songs eventually.

Lots of people were nice and lots of people were crazy at the Menninger Clinic. I remember an older girl, well into her twenties. When you are a teen people who are twenty-five seem old. She was a "Cousin It" type, the sort who'd be locked in the attic. Like Mr. Rochester in *Jane Eyre*. She liked to name drop. She'd like to pull you aside to point out prominent families. There was someone named Ed, and whenever we were sawing wood they had to make sure he was properly dressed because he was so disturbed and he'd be out in a Canadian-like winter in his underwear. He would just not notice.

There was one girl—Cindy, who was only a few years older, and she was really disturbed. She would walk around in a daze. She was inclined to mischief and violence. She would come up to people and she would speak in a monotone, and tell everyone she loved them in a hoarse, flat voice. Sometimes she'd kiss you on the cheek. Then she'd walk away in a trance. She always had a blank kind of stare. You never really knew when she'd do this. She'd come back later that day and say she hated you. And then kick you. After the first time you knew to dodge when she'd get near you, dodge her kicks and her kisses. She did this to a priest named Father Jack, and he kicked her back. Father Jack wore those heavy old steel tip oxfords, and when he kicked her she staggered. She deserved it.

Father Jack was there for alcoholism, of course. He always made me laugh. The teenagers, Ken, Alan, and Lucia, who took me up, for some reason they were always put in different activities from me. I was always separated from the other teens and put in the same activities and exercise class as Father Jack who was in his fifties. I never understood why and I never asked. I was only a year younger and I should have been in the youth group but at the time I didn't feel left out.

It didn't occur to me then but I wonder about it now in retrospect. I don't even know if the other young people *were* in an exercise class. The lady who led it was a very chirpy young lady, someone you'd hire to do

"Romper Room." The priest would be mean to her and she'd say "Now Father Jack …" She handed it really well and looking back I admire her. I was in an arts and craft class too, me and him and a girl who was in her twenties. They put in my file they were impressed with my drawing.

Father Jack wasn't much of a mentor but he sure made me laugh when I was only seventeen. He said things beyond politically incorrect, even for that time. I'm sure he said some things just to get me laughing. He was a mean old drunken 1940s type father, the kind who would have terrified the altar boys and would be screaming all the time. Father Jack would say the worst things—politically incorrect doesn't even begin to describe it—and he was always swearing. Even so, he always making me laugh.

We didn't have any chores at Menninger because it was more like a hospital. We did have outings. They'd get us up in the morning during the day and they'd take us out, sawing wood. Apparently, it was supposed to be therapy. You got your aggression and anger out. Maybe it worked on some people, I don't know. We'd saw wood with two-handed saws. Then we'd go to the canteen and have donuts and coffee.

I didn't have my first cup of coffee until after I left Menninger. It was sometime in Chicago. I was always in trouble and always losing my privileges. I behaved badly. One thing about Menninger is that they let me watch TV, even if I lost privileges they just restricted me to the ward. I didn't get to go eat with everyone in group dining. With bad behaviour I just waited it out. You get used to stuff like that. I'd read a book or play with my portable chess set.

I remember there was an aide who was a retired sergeant. I threw a log at him and then I didn't get to saw logs anymore. When I was behaving and in favor and worked my way up, I did get to go on outings with the teenagers. Ken and Alan and I went to the Beacon Public Library. I wanted to go because they'd show black and white movies and I liked historical films.

Mr. Cushenberry had been an aide at Menninger forever. He was a fine gentleman. He was so big he had to have his shoes custom made. He'd played for the Negro Leagues in baseball back when they were called that.

He taught me to play pool well at the canteen and we had a good time. He said, "Mark, you have a lot of talent." He was so good to me. I'd gotten good at ping pong at the medical center where I'd been before. A young aide taught me that and we played a good deal and I kept playing it at the Menninger Clinic. Mr. Cushenberry did shame me. He used to think a man is only as good as his word. I got caught lying and he shamed me, wouldn't speak to me, and quit playing pool with me. I felt bad. The day before I left the Menninger Clinic he took me for a walk around the grounds. That was his way of saying goodbye.

At Menninger they did ink blot tests, and puzzles, and something with matchsticks, and they had me draw things, and asked questions where you could get into trouble if you didn't pay attention to things. I was tested at Menninger for IQ and it did my self-esteem some good. I had an IQ of 150. It was a real boost, even though I don't believe in them. They can devastate a young person's self-esteem before they even have a chance, and they aren't even reliable. I sure wouldn't want to take another IQ test because apparently, they vary.

I was on some sort of sedative at night at the Menninger Clinic, and it didn't do anything negative to me. Those weren't the days of heavy medication. I had a number of problems and everybody did their best for me. A psychiatrist at Menninger wasn't on my team but he took an interest in me, and I appreciated it. He was a gentleman. The other psychiatrists were like they came from central casting, wearing shabby old sports jackets and nothing they wore matched, but they didn't care.

My doctor was like that. It was the early '70s, and they'd have bellbottom trousers on, but a twenty-year-old sports jacket with thin lapels. They looked like clowns. Nothing about their clothes worked. But this psychiatrist was so distinguished—out of fashion but with a great wardrobe from the early 1960s. He was real dignified and I can still picture him. Clothes like that have been in fashion for decades. I remember him in the winter; he had on an overcoat and like looked like Dad.

Dad got his overcoat at Saville Row in London. The psychiatrist was like that. He was elegant with beautiful clothes and he made an impression, and so polite, and he'd stop and ask me how I was getting along. I got the feeling he treated me with more dignity than the doctors who called me Mr. Landis, even though he called me Mark. I did like it that my own psychiatrist called me Mr. Landis. I was only seventeen and no one had called me Mister before, and I liked that. He would visit me once a week and I'd go for a walk with him.

They took us on outings at the Menninger Clinic. The boys went on separate outings than the girls. We went to all kinds of places, like museums. There was a man, Darryl, who was not just an aide, but someone who did other things, too; maybe he taught shop or something like that. He was a nice guy. I do remember the first time that I'd ever been in a thrift store and I got a couple of old art books there. I had to ask Darryl to pay because we weren't allowed to handle money.

I often didn't get to go on the outings because of bad behaviour. On those times I had to eat on trays and not go down to eat with the others. One thing they did was Friday night movies. I saw *The Sting* and *The Last Detail*. They also showed movies on weekends because they had a theater on the grounds, and I believe I always got to see those. Most people got to see the movies, except those under constant surveillance in case they might kill themselves. But there was only one person like that. We saw *Westworld* which was all right and we saw *The Way We Were*, which I hated, and I left because it was such a sickening movie. My psychiatrist forbade all his patients from seeing *The Exorcist,* which had just come out. See what a great psychiatrist he was? Another doctor did let his patients see it, but I missed it, because I was on trays. I saw it a few years later but it didn't make a lasting impression on me.

The complaints I have were the medications I had to take during the day. Primum non nocere is Latin for 'do no harm.' This does not apply to psychotropic drugs. I suppose they help some. At least it's not permanent like a lobotomy. There is no simple solution to anything, but those medications almost killed me. People aren't supposed to be happy all the time. Oliver Sacks uses the term "soul destroying," and "a spiritual death" and medication was like that for me. For a lot of people meds make them sleepwalk through life. What could they have done to Anne of Green Gables if she'd been going on flights of fancy? They wouldn't have locked her up or anything. They would have given her all kinds of drugs. When I left Menninger, they gave me a going away card that I still have. Lucia put down "draw long and well." John, who was from a rich family wrote, "the artist's hands speak the words the artist lips cannot utter."

After I was released in the 1970s all my friends from the Menninger Clinic came to see me, to have a little vacation. They'd gotten into a halfway house program, so they had more privileges and had more freedom. They took Amtrak to do a shopping trip in Chicago and they came to see me. They stayed at the La Salle, an old hotel. It was nice at the time but gone now. The boys went home afterwards, and Lucia decided to stay to do some shopping. I had one or two obligations that day. The film appreciation society was showing a film and, in those days, if you didn't see it you'd miss it. Not like today. Apparently, I wanted to see the film more than her.

I thought she'd go back to the hotel, but she showed up at my door saying she had to leave. My apartment was a tiny little place that looked out at a brick wall, something the school found for me in 1974. She came in and she was so mad, throwing things around yelling about the hotel. Back then people didn't have credit cards, only privileged young people had them. She had a credit card, but she managed to get it cancelled that week. I think probably what happened was that the hotel called her parents.

She showed up with all these bags. She'd just let herself go wild shopping. She had all these packages at my apartment. She bought an expensive pair of boots and was sad because she had broken up with her boyfriend. After she threw her tantrum she calmed down and we sat around and watched TV and stayed up all night and talked until five in the morning watching "The Late Show" and "The Late, Late Show." I remember we got lucky that night because the last thing we watched was "The Adventures of William Tell" until cartoons started. Lucia did most of the talking. She was a friend. I showed her how to take the bus to the airport. She was impressed with me. I went to the airport with her and helped her with her packages and she'd bought so much stuff we had to send some things on. She just went back to Topeka. She was living in a halfway house program at the time and she would have been twenty-one. I talked to her on the phone a couple times after that, but it was so expensive to call someone back then.

After I left the Menninger Clinic, I missed them all terribly. I missed them a lot in the 1980s. Ken got in touch with me recently and reminisced with me. It shook me up when I got a letter from him. It had been fifty years so it was emotional to talk to him, and I still haven't spoken to him on the phone, and only through email.

Ken sends me nice stuff all these years later, like stamps, KGB stuff, Russian medals, and even clothes. Once he sent me a *Playboy* pin that Dad really would have liked. Ken did well—he had his own little exploration company. He was a stockbroker for a while too when he was young. I saved some money when I was twenty-five. It was like a couple thousand dollars, and he helped me invest it. He was clever and he helped me make a few thousand dollars. These brokerages don't exist anymore because they merged with something else. I had no success as an artist because I was unreliable and inconsistent, so things like that helped me get by. I didn't get Social Security until 1987.

When I was eighteen and wanted to leave the Menninger Clinic they told my mother that I would be in institutions of some sort my whole life; I couldn't manage and needed a hospital. That was their prediction. I did end up in another one for a year, and a housing project. At Menninger, boy did they predict a gloomy future for me. I did keep going to school and dropping out. But at the time Mother went along with me and let me leave and go to school. The Menninger Clinic wanted me to go into a halfway house program, but they didn't think I'd be accepted because of my bad behavior from time to time.

When I left Menninger, I was an ungrateful teenager. I have

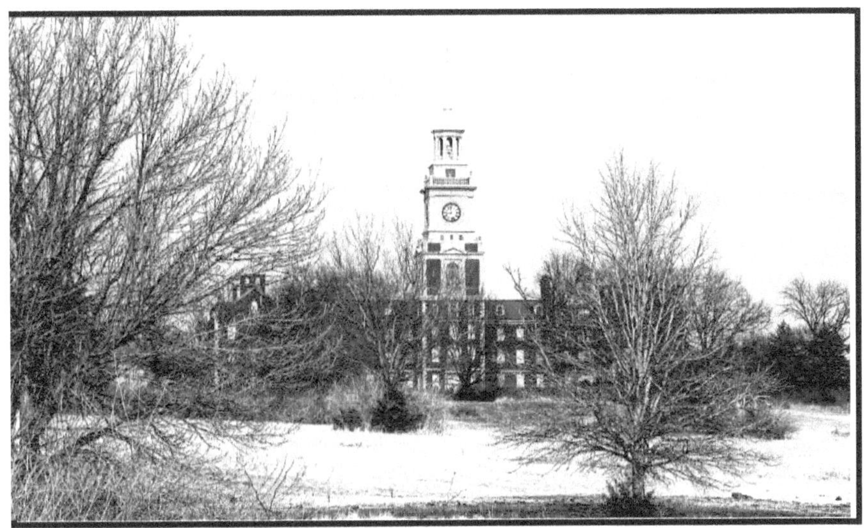

Menninger Clinic Clocktower. Photo: Emily Cowan of abandonedks.com

nothing but good things to say about that place now. I didn't appreciate them enough. I was interviewed by a psychiatrist before discharge, but I was sick of those places. The questions he asked me were so personal and I was a teenager and I got upset. I do remember the doctor saying, "If you walk out of here, I won't qualify you for benefits." I did anyhow. Wasn't too smart of me because Mother had to go to a lot of trouble filling out tons of forms. Took about a year.

When I got out of the Menninger Clinic, they wrote me letters and I ignored them. They did follow up with my Mother and called to see how I was. I didn't answer their phone calls or fill out forms. I just left and was just happy to have my own really small apartment in Chicago with a window that looked onto a brick wall. It didn't bother me because I had a black and white TV and an imagination. No one was yelling at me about things, like "If I let you stay up to see the end of the show then I have to let everyone."

The Menninger Clinic kept calling my mother to be sure I had money to live on. Social Security also kept sending letters for me to have an appointment. Mother was mad because of what I was putting her through. No one likes being yelled at by their mother. When I was twenty she didn't care. When I wasn't around she could let it go. When I was gone if a problem wasn't immediate she didn't think of it. She dealt with things when they came up. Like when I came back in 1986. It ended up being good because she got VA benefits for me because of Dad. I was just at the poverty guidelines even after the VA benefits, but they helped me get through a long time. In the movie *Door to Door* Bill Porter says that he is a salesman because he doesn't want to be on disability. But it's a movie though. I doubt he's quite as good as he seems. But initially I was getting by. I supported myself fine until my next breakdown at age thirty-one. In the mid-1990s I couldn't support myself without moving home. I sold a painting from time to time but not enough to pay the bills.

The Menninger Clinic used to contact me about studies. My conscience bothers me about it now, that I didn't do anything for them. They were a fine place. I'm ashamed. The Menninger Clinic moved to Houston in the early 2000s and that's so odd to me. It can't be the same. I'm sure it's still a fine place. You tend to sentimentalize things as you get older. We are all a bit embarrassed by some of the things we did when we were younger, but mainly we remember the pleasant things, like the friends we make. I saved so many of the things from the Menninger Clinic. I found old books they gave to everybody, like *What Every Teen Needs to Know About Drugs*. They didn't have to worry about that stuff with me though, just the things that were wrong with me—I don't know if it was congenital or what—but I always had them. When I got out I managed to do all right.

The Menninger Clinic in Kansas is abandoned now. You can see photos online. Everybody had pleasant memories of the place, at least the ones who wrote comments online. Some people were there before me in the 1960s, but most were there in the 1990s. Nobody had anything bad to say. Looking at the old photos I remember walking up and down those halls. I remember them being wider, but you know how memory is. They ought to save some of the buildings—it's a historic place. I never got locked up there like I did at the medical center. But then again, even at UMC I was never treated inhumanly by anyone.

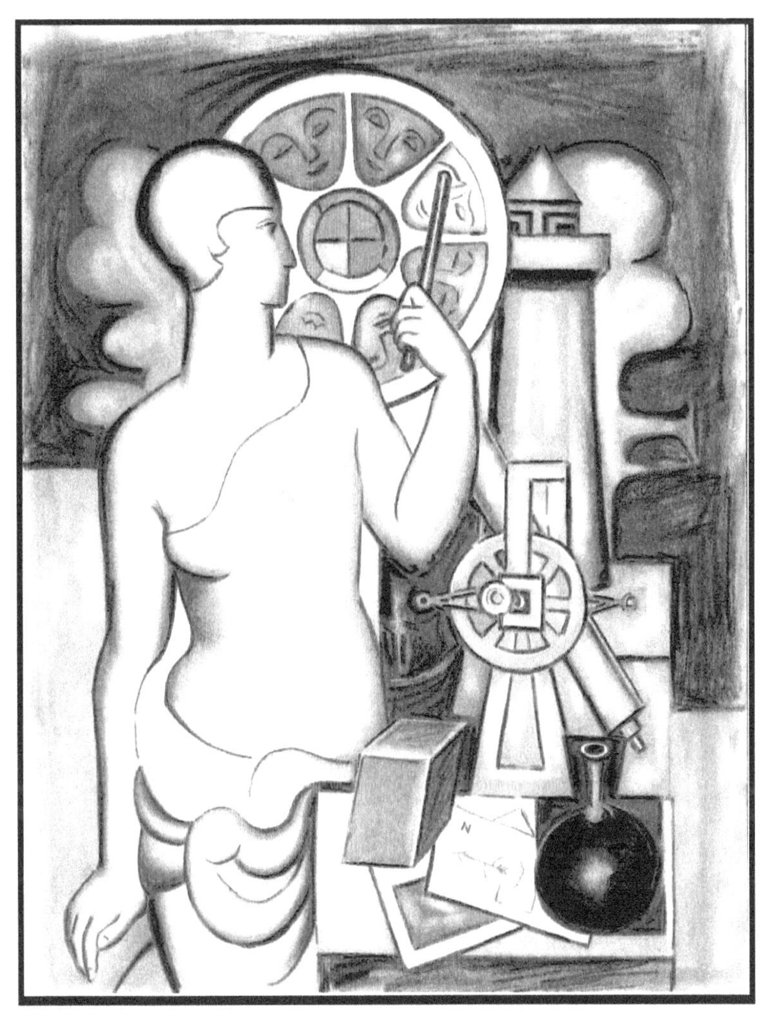

Illustration by Mark Landis

<u>8</u>

CHICAGO

After the Menninger Clinic one of Mother's friends told her I should go to The School of the Art Institute of Chicago because it was one of the top universities and had prestige. Matisse had lectured there once. He didn't look like the artists in the movies and wore a proper three-piece grey suit—quite respectable looking. Unfortunately, sending me there turned out to be a bad idea. It was the wrong school for me because it didn't really teach me to do anything, and just focused on interpretation. A no-nonsense school would have shown me how to be an illustrator, which is what I wanted.

It was an adventure being on my own. Like any young person I was glad that I got to stay up as late as I wanted to and watch whatever I wanted, with no one telling me what to do. The school found the apartment for me, the cheapest I could get, on North Dearborne Avenue, next to a church. It was old and had an elevator that I didn't trust and my apartment was on the second or third floor. I lived in a tiny room with a refrigerator and sink and a narrow gas oven. I never used it because I was afraid of lighting it. There was a payphone in the lobby downstairs and Mother and I would talk for five minutes on Friday nights.

The Chicago Art Museum was a big grey stone building with arches and a bronze sculpture of a lion, and the Art Institute was in back. You could get to the school in two ways: through the front or you could go through the museum. There was a door in the back. When I think about it now it seems really backward because there wasn't much security back then. I believe the door was open, although there may have been a guard. There weren't any complicated push button locks in the 1970s. They were doing a lot of construction at the time when I was there so I don't remember it all very clearly.

In photography they didn't teach you to do anything, just said things like "let yourself go." I don't know how I managed. I never could think of anything I wanted to take a photograph of. On the other hand it's probably just as well that I was sent to the Chicago Art Institute, which was too lax when I was there. I complain about it because there wasn't a lot of structure and there were no grades too, but at that time I probably couldn't have applied myself at a different school. If something didn't interest me I simply wouldn't do it.

In those days the art department was next door to the Goodman School of Drama, a famous drama school, which is now called The Theater School. All the nice young people, the art students and theater students, were together in the cafeteria, although they kept to their own tables. The actors would arrive still wearing their costumes. It was a little like the show *Fame*. When something is well written it seems real to you, so the school was a little like the television show, but not exactly. I made friends with one group and took photos of them.

At the institute I took a class in film making. I dropped it after three weeks, but I've certainly kept the film appreciation. We had "Super 8" groups we were placed in to make short films. All the films then were strange and experimental. I wanted to make one called the life of St. Laurence; we could have borrowed the costumes from Goodman's and there were lots of neoclassical buildings around Chicago that would have worked, but the other students didn't like my idea so I dropped the class. I'm still thinking of making a short, animated film of St. Laurence, a bit like *Davey and Goliath*. It would have some comic relief. Sam, who did the *Art and Craft* documentary, said he'd help me make it and we did do a little bit of work on it.

In Chicago I made friends with someone named Raymond, not to be confused with my friend Raymond who was a quadriplegic I met much later on. When the course first began teachers would have people say something about themselves. When it was my turn, I lied. Chicago was cool and fashionable in 1976, so I said that I was from Washington, DC, a place I was familiar with, instead of Mississippi, even though it wasn't like

I was actually from Mississippi; I was only there three years, then in hospital, but I didn't want people to think Mother was one of the people in that crowd in *To Kill a Mockingbird*. It was disreputable back then. Afterwards, Raymond came up to me. He had one of those student employment scholarships and he worked part time to pay for school and worked in the office where he had access to things. He came up to me later and said, "Mark, you're not from Washington."

He said he knew I was really from Mississippi, but he assured me he wouldn't tell anyone. He protected me from the curse of my coolness, which was good of him. He once knew it was my birthday and didn't tell anyone and I thought he was a good friend. Raymond would also support me in art critiques. Not long ago he got in touch with me. He found all these amazing pictures of Matisse lecturing. He is a successful publisher of limited-edition art posters.

When I was twenty, and still in my first year at Chicago, I made an enemy, so I had to leave. I didn't mean to make an enemy—I acted on impulse which caused the whole situation—but I did, and people like that can set out to sabotage you. This person was a friend at first, and he worked at the school. One day when I was visiting him, I saw faculty ID forms lying around and I lifted one.

I went back and had an ID card made for myself, and from there I went into the museum speciality sections and asked to look at all sorts of things. The boss found out and got mad at him, and made a sarcastic remark that insulted his intelligence, and because he was humiliated, he made a career out of making things hard for me. This friend devoted his life to revenge, much like the Alfred Hitchcock episode where cops want someone out of town so they enforce every petty thing on the books, like jaywalking, so it's impossible to stay there.

I can't remember his job. He was like a monitor, some kind of security position, and he could make it impossible for me to use a dark room at a certain time, and he found various ways to harass me and make things hard. I can see his point of view. Perhaps I deserved it for masquerading as a faculty member to see private collections, although all he did was get yelled at. I had seen too many episodes of "To Catch a Thief" with Robert Wagner, which I used to watch every evening in Chicago. With all of this going on I just couldn't have stayed there any longer. Like the Hitchcock movie, he ran me out of town by persecuting me. Aside from this it was cold in Chicago, so I went to San Francisco.

Before I left Chicago I did see a psychiatrist because it was booked for me. Mother told me to go because she was tired of them bothering her. Back then the Freudian school was in it its infancy, and although it is out of favor now, it was fashionable back then. He asked me all kinds of personal questions—you can use your imagination—and made me incredibly angry. I do remember him saying that if I didn't cooperate he wouldn't help, but I considered the questions extremely inappropriate so I didn't care and I left in a huff. You can always find a wealth of quotes by Alexander Pope and Lord Chesterfield that mean something. Lord Chesterfield said, "Those who want it most, like it least." Teenagers who need your advice and counsel most are the very one who like it least. And that's how it was with me back then. You're unrealistic and impractical when you're young and I thought there were all kinds of ships to sail. He didn't give me a diagnosis and Mother didn't care until she needed to apply for benefits; she hadn't even asked me how it went.

When I was around Mother noticed things, but if I wasn't she could put me out of her mind. Social security had contacted me several times after I'd been released from the Menninger Clinic, but I was young and I'd ignored their letters. A point they make in the film *Door to Door* is that the main character doesn't want to go on disability, he wants to work. I'm not as heroic as Bill Porter apparently. The only reason I didn't put in the effort to apply for disability is because by that point I was sick of seeing doctors. It wasn't until 1986, when I was 33, and came back to Mississippi that Mother applied on my behalf because she was angry that I didn't have any money and was a financial burden on her.

At first, I didn't receive it as they said I wasn't disabled prior to age 22 and they denied my claim for Childhood Disability Benefits "based on lack of evidence." Mother wrote to get a lot of my records so the Social

Security Administration would reconsider my application for disability benefits. She told them I had never had a job, had been sick and disabled, not able to support myself, and that the Menninger Foundation told her I should be committed. I don't consider myself disabled. I probably do have some challenges, but it's so subjective. When I was younger, and now too for that matter, I was unemployable. I was very unreliable and inconsistent and the very few jobs I had did not last longer than a couple of weeks. I had no self-discipline. If there was something I wanted to see on TV I stayed home and I watched it. At one point I did support myself as a hack artist. Inking cells is how I started out and it was drudgery. Naturally the quality of my work deteriorated because it was so boring. You have to suffer to be allowed to do backgrounds or something more interesting.

In the end I'm glad I left Chicago. I was happier in San Francisco—much, much, happier. It was better weather, I made friends, and it worked out, as it so oft does with Kismet. Time and chance our lives determine.

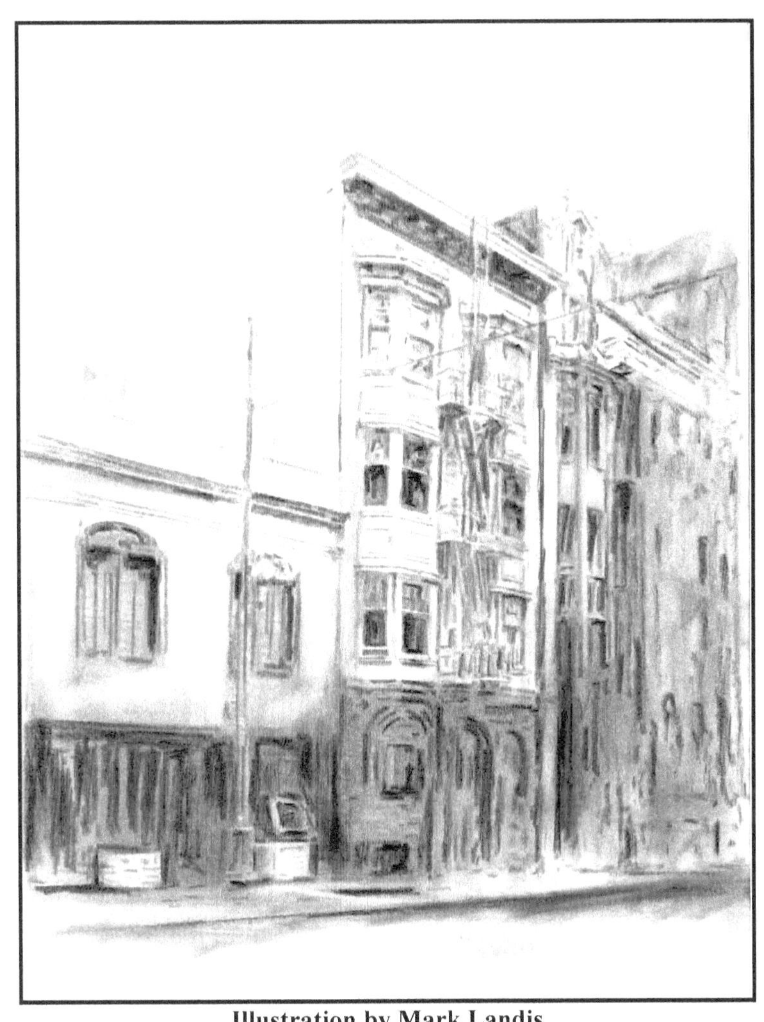

Illustration by Mark Landis

2

SAN FRANCISCO

In 1976, when I was twenty-one years old, I transferred to the San Francisco Academy of Art and moved to California. San Francisco was beautiful and I liked it very much. I took a bus from the airport to Union Square and it was all very exotic and interesting, and reminded me of shows I'd watch, like "Police Story" and "Police Woman"; it was just like one of those crime TV shows, with the shifty drug dealers and criminals, really racy street walkers and "Superfly" type guys on street corners—nothing I'd ever seen before in real life.

Mayor Moscone must not have been a good mayor to let the city be that way, and it wasn't gentrified yet, but as a twenty-year-old I was fascinated by it and I found it exciting. Then, as now, it was a popular runaway city for young people. There were many people who looked like hippies but weren't; in the '70s they weren't really spreading love, they were just aimless young people asking for money. There is a documentary made about it called *Streetwise*, because it was such a popular runaway city for young people back then. The young runaways would come up to me and try to con me and ask me for money, as if I'd have any—I was their age.

The downtown was okay and had nice people. Back then people used to ride cable cars for transportation before it became all tourism in the 1980s, but I remember riding it to get to school from where I lived. I ended up living in San Francisco for ten years, although I did move away for a little while, and I never actually saw the Cliff House. I painted pictures of it but never went in. I also didn't go into Candlestick Park either, although I'd often pass it on the bus.

The school didn't have a place for me to stay, although I think they tried to help some. I ended up staying first at an inexpensive hotel that had weekly rates. They used to have these paperbacks for tourists, and they'd have a chapter on cheap places to stay and I stayed at one of the places they recommended.

To find an apartment I had to get a newspaper. It was at Marquard's, a cigar and liquor shop right on the corner of O'Farrell and Post that I met Antonio Torres. His brother owned it. It had a big black and white marquee that read *Marquard's Little Cigar Store* and it was very popular. I used to walk past it all the time.

Mr. Torres and his family had immigrated to San Francisco from Spain in 1915 and he was a self-made millionaire property owner. At the time he owned several buildings and at one time had owned a hotel. He knew right away that I was new to the city and had probably come there to go to school, and although he was sixty-six and I was twenty, we hit it off right away. I don't know why. You couldn't have spoken to him about literature. I explained to him I had trouble finding a place to live that I could afford, and he befriended me and took a fatherly interest in me.

Mr. Torres got me an apartment at 967 Sutter Street, in a building next to one he owned. He was friends with the owner. It was in a basement apartment with a little window that looked out on the street. It was a small two-story building built on a hill. There was a large apartment downstairs that was partly storage, and my apartment opened in the back onto a nice garden. The basement part had at one time been an architectural planning and drafting office. The downstairs was very much dilapidated when I was there and had an abandoned look, the way Menninger's does now, sitting empty. The building is still there and when I saw a picture online it is very much the same, although I'm sure it has likely been much renovated.

Mr. Torres was a self-made man who had uplifted himself. He was always up to something. I didn't know about it at the time, but Mr. Torres had once served eighteen months for tax evasion. He'd gone to San Quentin and the California Men's Colony. At that time sentences were sometimes indeterminate, but he was let out to fight fires. He said one day they just walked up to some of them and asked, "How would you like to fight some fires?" After that he bought the building he lived in. He talked like someone in *The Untouchables*. He would have had the same likes and dislikes and prejudices as a white man from the 1940s, very much an Archie Bunker type. He was that way until the end and did not in any way alter his manner of speech or opinions and feelings with the changing times. He would say some things and have some violent prejudices and his mouth was even worse than Father Jack's.

Mr. Torres taught me to play billiards at Palace Billiards. He taught me "three cushion billiards"—the kind where there are no pockets, which was still played at the time, although not by anyone my age. We'd play cards together too. Mr. Torres introduced me to some people who owned a Chinese restaurant at the corner and I would often go there for my meals. They were very nice and they befriended me. One thing led to another, and we started playing Mah Jong and Chinese chess together. The owner gave me my first Chinese chess set. I later bought a good one in Chinatown, and I still have the one he gave me. I don't use the one I bought because it's a show piece.

In San Francisco the TV Guide ruled my life. If "Tennessee Tuxedo" was on, I couldn't make it to school. I remember skipping class and racing home to catch the after school special. It was then that I saw Rosanna Arquette in *Mom and Dad Can't Hear Me*. Needless to say, it didn't occur to me that forty years later we would be friends. I didn't like watching game shows, and I could usually manage to find something else on, like an old Western. In the cities I lived in there would always be a channel showing old movies or reruns, or PBS. I'd often turn it on which is why I know the old children's TV shows.

"Sergeant Preston of the Yukon" would come on early in the morning on Saturdays, which is how I'd start my day. The school was built on a hill and I remember a huge archway and there was a Rivera mural over it, and we had lockers in there. I thought the Diego Rivera mural was ugly. It made no impression on the young people—it was just something that was on the wall and we ignored it. Despite the classes I missed I got very close to completing my degree, but something happened which prevented it.

Mother got married three years after Dad died, in 1978. For all her faults my aunt was around a lot and Mother had friends, so she wasn't lonely, but she said that she'd have security if she got married again. I hadn't met my new stepfather, because it's not like a situation comedy where mothers are worried about their children's reaction. She just sort of told me she was marrying, but I was grown up so it was all right by me. She wanted me to come home to give away the bride. Mother never had any confidence in me. I was studying photography and yet she didn't let me take the photos. That was just Mother being Mother.

My stepfather went out of his way to be nice to me. He knew I wasn't going to be around for long. They had cable TV, with clear reception, and it was the first time I'd watched TV without a ghost. Like a lot of young people I ended up just reading and watching TV—cable TV was just so new for me. I read a book at the same time since Mother instilled in me you should always try to improve yourself. You can read an entire book but even if you only take away one small thing it was worth your $3.95. And you can always find new meaning in the classics; that's why they're timeless. And I love when I find a new book when I was looking for something else in a bookstore or library.

It was a big mistake going home, one that a lot of young people make. I remember one Saturday afternoon when I lived in London as a child, I watched *A Tree Grows in Brooklyn*. It was a great movie. In the film the mother tells her daughter that she can work for a while then go back to school, but she cries, "Everybody says that and they never do." It was true. When I left San Francisco art reflected life and although I had less than a semester to get my degree, I didn't go back to school. I got into the pattern of watching TV until the late, late show and then slept late, although I liked daytime TV more than evenings. Other than read while I watched TV, I didn't really do anything when I was living with my mother and stepfather. I became a slacker, although they didn't call it that in the '70s. There was no one to make me to do anything.

After six weeks I went to Atlanta and thought I'd go to their Art Institute and finish the degree. The idea was that I'd be closer to home. One of my friends told me I'd like it but I'd acquired too many bad habits. This time Mother paid for me to take a plane and I got a bus at the airport and a paper and walked around until I found a place to live. I found a cheap apartment with everything in one room, a sink in the corner and the bathroom down the hall. I had some money I saved to live on. It got awfully hot there. I didn't have air conditioning and I sank into a pattern of idleness and sloth. I was there from 1978-1979. Somehow, I managed to survive.

After I'd been in Atlanta for a year Mr. Torres called me and one thing led to another and I thought, I liked it better in San Francisco and had more friends… it just seemed more like my sort of place. I never made any friends in Atlanta, just sat around, and so I went back and ended up living in Mr. Torres's building from 1979-1986. It was also a basement apartment and he let me live there for free for doing other little things. I typed letters for him because his grammar was terrible. I also used to kind of take care of Mr. Torres's dogs that lived in the garden. He was friends with waiters at Original Joe's, which mainly served steaks and things like that. They would save the leftovers and give them to Mr. Torres for his dogs, and I went by there once or twice to pick them up. I took care of Mr. Torres' old Doberman to help him out, and I got along with him, but the one who replaced him was just a bad dog.

Some people are habitual criminals, bad ones, and the dog would have been like that. If he was on a *Lassie* episode, he'd be the one sneaking out at night killing sheep. He would frame *Lassie*. There are certain kinds of juvenile delinquents beyond hope. One day he had to take the dog away and I didn't ask for the details. He said the dog knew he was leaving. He'd dug up the sofa.

Mr. Torres thought I'd be upset about it, but I wasn't. I do like dogs. Dad had a little dog when he was small, he had lots of pets, but we moved around a lot so we couldn't have a pet when I was growing up, so although I like dogs I just don't have much experience with them other than Mr. Torres' dogs. I don't remember much wanting one, or if I did, I don't remember. A puppy did follow me home once and I wouldn't have minded keeping him. It kind of gets me in the heart. I did do something good for him because I lived near a police station so I took the puppy there and a young officer took him.

I'm pretty good knowing '60s music because of living in San Francisco. I often watched TV with extremely poor reception because of the hills and you could often not see an image, only static. I listened to the radio at the same time because there was a station that only played oldies from the '60s and they used to give away a lot of prizes and run contests. Mr. Torres had a special phone deal in the '80s and you could get extra features like speed dialling—things we take for granted now but it was state-of-the-art then. Because of the speed dialling feature, which most people didn't have, I could just keep pushing the button until I won the contest. I used to win a great deal of things that were of no use to me— like a bike. I didn't use it, but it was a great present. I gave a lot of things away as gifts. Companies were always promoting stuff, gourmet things like candies and baskets. Occasionally I won something I wanted, but mostly I gave everything away. Of course, I ended up hearing a lot of the '60s music because of this.

There was a place called the Carlton Hotel, at 1075 Sutter Street, owned by Diane Feinstein who was the mayor the entire time I lived there. She later went on to become a senator. I remember Mr. Torres used to take me there to the restaurant, Kam's Oak Room, for my birthday and Thanksgiving dinner.

Mr. Torres owned two rather valuable buildings. He'd have been about a millionaire in the 1980s, wealthy but not rich. He always had little deals going. He was in WWII, and he was particularly bitter sending money home for various things, and his family member was using it for a no-good boyfriend. Mr. Torres was a wheeler dealer right until the very end. He avoided the crippling paralysis of retirement, that trope. I never owned an art gallery at any time, although some articles say I did. Years later, when I was travelling around people would ask me about it, and probably I did say that I'd owned one at some time or other, which caused confusion. When I was a philanthropist and donating paintings I was often asked about my business and I'd say various things, from investments to art dealer—always an art collector—and I may have given that impression. But Mr. Torres sometimes used my name on things involving his businesses and schemes and deals and I was sometimes the owner on paper for real estate, so it might have been that my name is on something that I had nothing to do with. I did invest in one thing with Mr. Torres and lost all my savings. I had saved some money with one thing or another, about $10,000-15,000. I can't remember the exact amount. Whereas most people overestimate, I always underestimate. Any time I say a dollar amount it's almost always much more than that.

My friend Ken from time to time helped me make money in the stock markets, or I made a bit of money as a commercial artist, for lack of a better word. Mr. Torres and I were supposed to buy property together to build a house in Lake County, California but I lost all my money. I'm not mad at him because he asked me to go up there a couple times to look and I just didn't feel like it. He died a few years later. I tested Mr. Torres beyond endurance, and so, I forgave him for the real estate thing a long time ago. I was never homeless, even if I only had a few hundred dollars in my pocket, although I was close to being so. It's a miracle I supported myself—I only had $100-200 in savings at best. I did however support myself, and because Mr. Torres was a good friend to me it meant I could stay in San Francisco for ten years.

I lived on Sutter Street, so I got to know all the art galleries. All of the best, established art galleries were on that street. I made friends with a couple of the dealers and so I was able to repair pictures for some of them, not the real expensive pieces. I started superficially touching up some paintings, but I wasn't clever and just used acrylics or whatever materials I could get at Woolworths or Michaels. I was certainly not a trained art restorer. One of the dealers was Chet Helms. I didn't know who he was at the time. Long after I left the city I saw him interviewed on PBS, saying he had been Janis Joplin's manager, but he had been just a seedy old art dealer to me. He was nice to me, and we got along well. Sometimes people would come in and try to talk to him about his days in music, and I remember him being sharp with someone because he was with a customer and didn't want to talk about that.

I had no interest in music so I certainly didn't care about his past. I painted pictures for him and the subject he liked best was paintings of the Cliff House at various times in history. I used pictures from a book. He sold them to tourists and I didn't sign them because I was a nobody. He also liked politically incorrect paintings of Black people, which is something he collected. There were also occasions that I rescued pictures. I could take a terrible, awkward, amateurish painting and I could make it presentable and make it attractive. I could take a child that looked painted like a ventriloquist's dummy and turn it into a Victorian angel, which takes considerable skill.

I did enter a prestigious artist's competition once at the Art Institute. I copied quite a good watercolor, an obscure painting, so there was no possibility the judges recognized it. It would have been one of the greatest artists of the century. I was, of course, rejected as I'd feared, which reinforced my belief that there was something I didn't understand about these competitions. When they rejected the painting, thinking it was only me who had done it, they were rejecting one of the greatest artists of the twentieth century. There's something I just didn't understand in this system, something wrong with it. However, I didn't feel too badly because I hadn't put much work into it, and I didn't have to pay an entrance fee because I was a photography student at the time. I'd even watched a good show while I'd worked on the watercolor, so I didn't really lose anything by trying.

Chet Helms' girlfriend was in her eighties, and was a mean, reformed hippie—a yuppie type—stingy, greedy, and upwardly mobile. I find with some people there's no moderation; they are one extreme or another. She was the most difficult person I ever dealt with trying to get paid, and I didn't like how she treated me, often thinking of little ways to humiliate me.

One thing led to another, and people would end up asking me to do things. I was commissioned to paint the portrait of two daughters of a socially prominent woman in San Francisco, and I worked harder on that piece than anything I had ever done before and since. I labored over it for many weeks. It was big, 16 x 25. I'd taken pictures first with my Pentax camera. When it was completed I showed it to Alma Gilbert, the director of the prestigious La Galleria on Sutter Street, which carried Maxfield Parrish paintings. She was the resident expert on his work. I had repaired paintings for Mrs. Gilbert in the past and she had gotten me the commission. Mrs. Gilbert said the painting was beautiful.

Later on, I received a large envelope from the woman who'd commissioned the piece with a card thanking me and saying the painting was beautiful and charming. People told me it was hanging over her mantepiece in her big house, some place near Palo Alto, although I can't remember exactly. Of course, along with the card I'd expected a check.

But after all that work she stiffed me! That was devastating for someone who was twenty-five. This was formative for me as a young man. Truly, it was always much harder collecting money from people than doing the actual paintings. You can't just ask for money; you have to be subtle, and I was young so I didn't have a lot of skill in that department, although I was better than many young people at being tactful. I lacked assertiveness, one of the things that the Menninger Clinic had noticed, and the doctor said that if I made any friends at all I'd always be taken advantage of.

That's why I started learning to make pictures fast. No one is faster than me. It's better to not be paid for something that took you a couple of hours than it is to not be paid for something that took you a few days or months. If there is one thing I want to be known for it is that, and it's what I would tell young artists: just do the work fast in case you aren't paid. What's amusing, is that although for years I thought the woman had stiffed me, not long ago when I was going through Mother's things I found that she had indeed sent a check. Mother had just forgotten to give it to me because she was distracted and upset by the hurricane.

I started illustrating for a newspaper in 1982 or 1983, The Examiner Chronicle, but my nature came out and I started hacking it out. I wasn't there long enough to get bored. I did ad illustrations for the ad agency that put advertisements in there, such The Emporium, which was a big department store. The woman was nice and she tried to have a good talk with me and help me, but I didn't change. I was just unreliable and they couldn't count on me.

I just barely got by with money, but somehow, I managed to. Whenever there was a gallery show I was invited to, I would go and stuff myself. Those were my best meals. I have joked that kids are freeloaders, but when you are young, naturally you will take free food. Mr. Torres knew most of the restaurant owners and other building owners, and when I was young I spent a good deal of my time getting free meals. One was a restaurant for pensioners. I remember being young and seeing them and wondering what I would be like at that age.

When I was in San Francisco I didn't see Mother for five years, and we only called on weekends when rates went down at, mainly Friday nights at 11:00. Mother didn't mind and put up with it. She would time the calls. If you had to say something you had to get it out of the way. I always called her on my birthday. Most students I knew did fly home once a year and it was usually at Christmas. There were a lot of holidays since the Menninger Clinic that I spent all alone, and many of my birthdays. Although I was sitting around in my little low rent apartment on holidays, I can't say I was depressed and feeling sorry for myself. I was glad to be independent and on my own, and it was better than a hospital with someone telling me to turn the TV off.

Some people might get down about the holidays because they almost think they are supposed to—it's suggestive. They weren't sad to me because they were special because of the holiday programming, which I looked forward to. Because of the special holiday rates, I had a long-distance call with Mother. She didn't send me gifts in San Francisco because it was too much trouble, although did send me a check after she was married, for maybe $20, nothing big, but that was sensible of Mother because she didn't know what to get me. Between my phone call with Mother and the Christmas films and television shows I wasn't unhappy.

Many things have changed through the years. Christmas isn't the same as it used to be because you can see holiday shows all year round.

I remember I bought my first suit in 1979 from Brooks Brothers in San Francisco. I thought it would be good for my self-esteem and it seemed to me that buying a suit somehow meant success and would help me. There was an older English gentleman working there. He seemed much older to me, although probably only in his sixties and younger than I am now, but he seemed real old to me at the time. He had such beautiful manners and kept calling me "Sir" which I really liked because I've always had a problem with poor self-esteem. He sold me a blue suit which I look dignified in, as opposed to the grey one I preferred. He sold me a couple of shirts and some ties to go with the suit.

The gentleman suggested I take the shirts and ties without paying and trusted me to come back and pay later. This was before young people had credit cards; older people did have them, but young people didn't, although of course my friends at the Menninger Clinic had them. Later on, I got a card in the mail saying my suit was ready and to come in at my convenience and I went back and paid for it. It always impressed me that this gentleman put his trust in me, a young man. Funny how sometimes you meet someone just once, you have a conversation with them on a train or something, just meet them for a moment and never see them again but you never forget them.

After I left for the last time, I used to miss San Francisco. It took a long time to get used to not being there anymore, but I don't miss it now. When I went back everything had changed so much; stores I was familiar with like Woolworths at the corner of Powell and Market, where the streetcar turned around, were gone. You could kind of recognize the buildings, but everything had changed.

Years later, when the San Francisco Art Institute was going to let me come back, they said I was a performance artist. I don't really think much about it. As far as art I like academic art, like the Victorian's art, and Mother did too. With the proper training and good school I may have been a good artist but I wouldn't do performance art.

In 1986 when I lost all my money because of Mr. Torres' investment, I ended up hospitalized for a little bit, not that losing the money was all that upsetting. I was upstairs at the San Francisco Public Library, an old, large building. They had kind of a ledge by the window near the stacks and people would sit there sometimes, and I suppose I was in kind of a bad way and had fallen asleep. Staff thought me a concern and they called an ambulance. I was taken to hospital and then social services got in touch with Mother, and someone took me to the airport and put me on a plane home. I was there for about a week or so and then I was seen by the local mental health and retardation services through Pine Belt. I went to South Mississippi Hospital for about four days, just for observation, then home again to my grandmother's house where my mother and stepfather lived. I didn't really get to know my stepfather until that time. He wasn't anything like Dad.

When I came back my stepfather wasn't as nice as when I first met him. It shook me up moving back in with him because things had changed so much. He thought I was a "four flusher" or a "blowhard"—a Walter Mitty type who just daydreamed. With time and reflection time heals all wounds but the scars are still there. Confucius used to say friendships broken can be mended, but like a China bowl, the cracks will show. My stepfather has been dead a long time, since 1997, and with time I can see his side of things, so I don't blame him. He was expecting a pleasant retirement and he already had to live with my grandmother who didn't like him, so things were already difficult for him living in my grandmother's house. I was the only one around for him to yell at and abuse.

He was like someone from central casting in *To Kill a Mockingbird*. He spoke like that. He was a retired army warrant sergeant and worked for the transportation department for the city of Jackson. He wasn't a gentleman like my father. Dad fit into modern society. But Stepdad was good to Mother, and he did leave her money. He never knew about my drawing and painting, and he never found out I was a secret philanthropist.

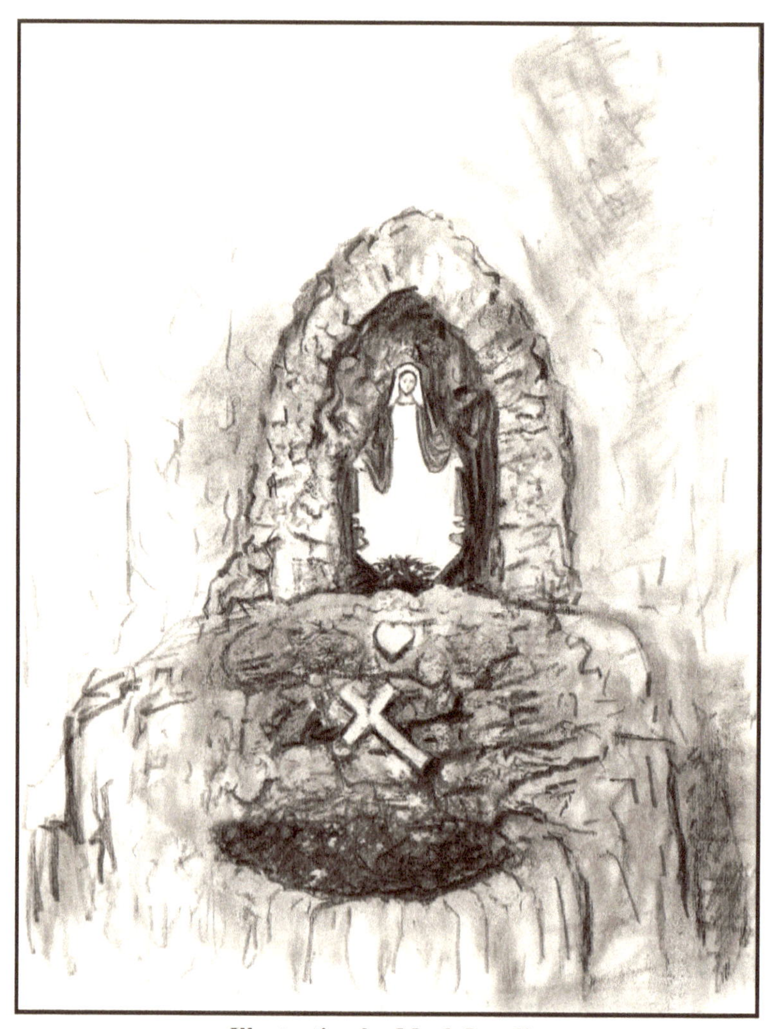

Illustration by Mark Landis

<u>10</u>

PINE BELT AND FEDERATION TOWERS

In 1987 I ended up at a Chronic Mental Illness (CMI) group home for the "chronically mentally ill" at age thirty, after a nervous breakdown. This was before the shake-up with political correctness ended up in names being changed. They had resources for people at the Regional Mental Health and Retardation Department Facility; but much has changed in thirty-five years in terms of political correctness and now it's known as Pine Belt Mental Health Resources. In 1989 Mississippi started getting rid of everything that wasn't politically correct. My group home was on Edwards Street in Hattiesburg and run by Pine Belt Mental Health and Rehabilitation. My first caseworker was Donna who was just twenty-two years old.

I don't know how I survived those twelve years in the group home. The name, "group home for the chronically mentally ill" basically tells you what it is. Some of those men in there really fit the bill. They kept changing their minds about how to refer to us. We used to be "clients," but they changed it to "consumers," and then they changed it back again. No one knew what was right to say. It was like *Man on a Tightrope*, when Adolphe Menjou is yelling at his subordinate because he kept getting all his terms wrong.

It was a big old house in poor repair. It was leased and so the repairs were the owner's responsibility. They did their best with what they were given so I have no complaints. There were a million rules, like there always are in places like that. The aides were poorly paid so you couldn't expect people who were in those jobs to have more than a high school education at best. They all had personalities, and some were nice and some weren't, and some were given to being petty tyrants over the silly little rules. Their personal frustrations would understandably be taken out on us.

That's just how things are. I recall one or two aides would think of a way to get to watch their favorite show and they were relatively subtle about it.

The meals were fine, and the aides were responsible for the cooking and a few ladies were talented cooks. After I left the home the mental health department meddled with things and wanted residents to cook simple meals, so they had the idea to teach them to cook. But if you knew those men like I did you wouldn't want anything to do with their meals. So often agencies make things worse, and that's the trouble with do-gooder types. Sometimes you should leave well enough alone.

The men in the group home were awful. It was overcrowded so I had a lot of roommates, and whenever someone wants to complain about a roommate, I say I can tell stories about guys in the group home that would shock them. They had no table manners and they behaved terribly during the meals. When I lived in London I was a few blocks from the zoo. They had a monkey's tea party and that's what meals in the group homes were like. Pine Belt was full of people like in the movie *Warrenville*, really irritating. They made me not like shaking hands.

I'm not particularly prone to physical affection, but if I can get away with it, when I greet people I go with a quick side hug or a tap on the shoulder. I'm not a hugger but if you know what filthy things those men did you wouldn't blame me. Ever since I got out of the group home I've hated shaking hands, and now I'm vindicated because we aren't supposed to do that any longer because of COVID. I'm glad it's gone out of fashion.

One of the guys at the group home was a human calculator. He could add or subtract huge numbers, which is sometimes an autistic phenomenon, nature's compensation. You could give him an algebra equation and he could solve it just like that. I'm not sure what was wrong with him, but he had a lot of problems. In other ways he was like a six-year-old. For example, at the dining table he'd just pick up food and just shove it in, or have trouble buttoning his shirt, little things like that. And then sometimes he'd surprise you with a sophisticated remark that would come out of nowhere.

We had chores there which was perfectly appropriate. The staff were all screws to us, like in prison movies, so we lied to them about doing those chores. Everybody did that. One week my chore was cleaning the common room, and I was vacuuming it. One of the staff, Shirley, came around and she grilled somebody over whether he'd done his chores. He said "yes," in his drawl, and she asked him what his chore was? He said, "the den" (which is what we called the common room), even though I was currently cleaning it. He wasn't exactly a master criminal.

I was too high functioning at the group home and I didn't really belong. It was a spiritual death. I got bullied from time to time, but people there didn't really hurt you. Things are worse now when even schools have metal detectors. People can be mean, and too often the solution was to prescribe drugs that caused people to behave like the characters in the movie *Awakenings*. They force people to take medications with bad side effects. The things I had to take. If you didn't swallow the pills, they'd make you take liquid medications which tasted awful.

At one time in history doctors killed more people than they helped. You had a better chance of living longer by staying away from doctors in the Middle Ages, and for a long time afterwards. Although they have learned from their mistakes, the medical profession sometimes still makes mistakes, like when they put me on Risperdal because I was a bad patient. It made me pace. I've had practically every drug through the years. Because I was a magician, I practiced my palming. I got fairly good at it, so I always got away with hiding my medications and throwing them out.

When I got out of the group home I told them I was still taking my medications but I had stopped; I just couldn't tolerate the side effects. They must help some people, but I think sometimes they do more harm than good. Mental health professionals need to ask if patients are actually happier on the meds prescribed or if they are just less trouble. I didn't take the pills again until later on in the late 1990s when they surprised me with blood tests which revealed I wasn't taking them. I was scared of losing my VA benefits, so I did what the social workers said. I hardly ever sold any pictures in those days, and I was travelling around as a philanthropist and needed the money, and Mother told me to live within my means. I'm a senior citizen now so they can no longer force me to take anything. The biggest thing to help me wasn't medication It was simply getting older.

It's extremely hard to look respectable in a group home. It's better than a jail, but not a whole lot better. I know a lot of people in jail are quite intelligent, so they probably take better care of themselves. The first time I grew a moustache was in the group home because you couldn't get in the bathroom—too many men and only one bathroom—so to save time I grew the moustache. But to be honest, I wouldn't cash a check from someone with a moustache who looked like me.

They called the day treatment place the "Club House." They bussed us there. Lots of movies sentimentalize mental health, but that's where movies are movies, and reality is a different thing. The mentally ill are just like everyone else. Some are nice, and some aren't. Just because someone is retarded doesn't mean they are nice.

Some were dangerous—you wouldn't want your daughter on the same bus as them. I wasn't afraid on the bus, but it was like an animal cage. Everyone was aged twenty to forty, but all acted like the worst behaviourally challenged children. The bus driver did her best, but there was only so much she ccould do. Fortunately, the ride wasn't long enough for trouble. The group home residents would arrive at day treatment and they'd just find a place to sleep. There was a hard bench and they'd pass out on it. Staff would make them get up to do activities but they'd just want to sleep. I used to like to play games—Scrabble and card games like Spades —because not too many people played chess and the ones who did were terrible. I played checkers as well. But then they decided games were unproductive and had us doing various activities that were supposed to be better therapy.

At the group home I went back to school at age thirty-five, for business administration and economics, just to get out of that place. I got my caseworker Donna on my side. My career choices were limited at the time, and I was thinking, maybe I could be an art teacher, so I asked my counsellor, Mrs. McGee, but she said I couldn't be a teacher because I wasn't assertive enough and I couldn't maintain any kind of discipline. I felt no one respected me—that's what got me to where I am. It wouldn't have happened to someone with good self-esteem. I went to the University of Southern Mississippi and I took proper classes, with lectures and desks, not like at art school. I was well into my thirties, so I had more discipline.

A lot of people wore caps in those days, and I did too, which made me look much younger than my age. On one occasion a couple of students sat next to me on the first day of class and asked me what high school I went to. I never told anyone that I wasn't their age, nineteen or twenty, and I got away with it which was fun. I got good grades because at thirty-five I could apply myself, but I eventually had to drop out. Back then an education was not cost prohibitive, maybe only a few thousand dollars, but I couldn't afford it. I got VA benefits and it was too much money, so I lost my Powell grant. That was when I started travelling around again being a philanthropist. Now people have huge debts coming out of school but that wasn't an option for me.

In 1990 Pine Belt dropped me because there wasn't much funding in those days, so I got myself out of the group home and into the housing project. On the last day, as I was leaving Pine Belt, I said, "Oh Lord, I have been delivered from the Egyptians!" That's when I moved into Federation Towers, which was a housing project. It was Section 8 housing, a federal program to help low-income people. I'd felt I was a third-class citizen in the group home but had worked my way up to second class citizen.

Federation Towers had fifty units and was in one of the worst parts of Hattiesburg, on Arnold Street. It was a white, three floor walk-up with metal balconies that faced the street. There were drug dealers in the old houses nearby and you'd see them out on their porches. I used to say hello to them and they'd say hello back. I had my own little apartment, and it was nice, not like housing projects on TV. Everyone living there was elderly or disabled. At first it was awkward living in a new place, but I started making friends, because I just treat people with disabilities the same as everyone else. I was happy there. The building is now supportive housing for the elderly and I believe it looks much the same from the outside.

Everyone living there was Black and mostly older, except for Raymond, who was a young quadriplegic. He was just twenty-three and the youngest person in the building. He referred to himself as a "quad." He was a nice young man who didn't deserve what happened to him. He'd had an accident on a worksite when he was young and the builder didn't have insurance. I was seven years older than him, but we were the only young white people—we had nothing else in common—but because of that we got quite close. We wouldn't normally have spent time together, but circumstances put us together. He depended on me, and we were friends for about seven years.

Raymond was disabled but he never got embittered like some people do. He did get depressed sometimes. He was once a big, strong guy, and it was hard to believe this little, withered guy in a wheelchair was once a burly construction worker. I would go out and buy him generic cigarettes because he said he didn't want to get addicted to anything good. He needed a lot of help. Sometimes he needed intimate help, and he wanted a man, so I'd help him, like with colostomy bags.

An aide would come in twice a week, and some were nicer than others. Poverty is not a character builder, and some aides were up to no good. I had to do Raymond's paperwork for him because he couldn't use his hands. He had a brother, but he was in Texas and couldn't help out very much. It turned out one aide kept changing the paperwork, so it said she worked more and therefore received more money, and then an investigator got involved; the aide practically attacked him. He eventually got a nice aide who was honest. Raymond was certainly a responsibility for me.

After I moved from Pine Belt I still returned to visit. The group home wasn't far from my new home in Federation Towers, only a few blocks, so I'd still go back and look in on everyone and play cards or ping pong. I haven't seen them since the early 1990s and I'm sure now they are all dead. A young guy who was quite irritating, always asking me for advice, was only twenty-three at the time—ten years younger than me. He is dead now, which shakes me up.

At Federation Towers the nice elderly ladies wouldn't eat their Meals on Wheels. Men would, but women liked their own cooking and wanted to make their own food, so they gave me theirs. I thought the food was okay. It saved me a lot of money and it was really kind of them. Mother made me live off of my disability allowance, and not live beyond my means. She had gone to a lot of trouble to get me that.

Later on, Raymond went to live with an aide for a year but as is often the case it didn't work out, and then he moved to a nursing home in Hattiesburg, and normally I'd go visit him once a month. Raymond was my only friend and I visited him for two years. The aides there were Black ladies, and they were all very nice, and the ladies who worked in the kitchen were nice too, and when I'd visit I'd get lunch. I missed Thanksgiving but a couple weeks later I went to visit Raymond. I had to walk in a bad storm. The staff got out a big Thanksgiving dinner for me, and Raymond and I had dinner together.

There was a while when I hadn't seen him because I'd been busy, and it was also a long walk from the Greyhound bus stop. When I finally went to see him, I showed up with a carton of cigarettes. Raymond wasn't in his usual room so I went to the desk to see where he had been moved to, and that's when an aide told me that Raymond had died. They felt bad no one had told me. I was so shocked I just walked out. It was terribly depressing.

When I got out of the group home in 1990, I was so thankful to God to get out I started going to church. I attended Holy Rosary Church on Dabbs Street, which was mainly a Black church, just a short walk from Federation Towers where I lived. It was a small, unassuming yellow brick building with a tiny white steeple. Sometimes white people came and everyone was polite, but you could tell they didn't really belong. The white people were just proud of themselves because of how unprejudiced they were, and everyone knew that the white people were there only to show off how progressive they were.

They accepted me because they knew I was from the group home and I think maybe at the start they liked that they could look down on me. There's probably something in Confucius or Benjamin Franklin—or psych 101—that if you help somebody out you sort of like them, because it establishes a deferential sort of friendship. That's what happened at Holy Rosary. It was the only place I was accepted as far as churches go. Everyone needs someone to look down on, and they could look down on me. I was a third-class citizen.

The people there were really nice to me, and in time they basically adopted me. I was a helper on occasion. Mrs. Hall got me to entertain at kids' parties, maybe six or seven of them. Mrs. Hall knew people within the church who had birthday parties for kids coming up, and because I was an amateur magician they got me to do children's birthday parties, and when they had a bazaar and a Easter egg hunt I was able to do a magic show for that, too. In Junior High I had done a magic show, and it had been a big success. The kids at Holy Rosary were very well behaved, and I never met a bad child at the birthday parties.

Back in the 1960s, when I was a kid, I was invited to a birthday party. That's when I was interested in magic. I was the only kid who could juggle so I got the bright idea to juggle eggs and I dropped one. I learned from that and I gave up on eggs as part of my routine. Don't get the impression I was much good—it was only a few parties. I mainly did card tricks, like sailing the card. I used to sail a card across the room and tie it into a fairy tale love story at parties. You never know when something will go wrong so you have to work it into the act, so you don't need to explain. Even though I wasn't much good as a magician, I thought, if something doesn't work (and even the greatest magicians have something go wrong) you need to have a good comeback line, just in case. That's why I always had "Prince of Patter" put on my business cards. I always had something clever to say.

At the church the Madonna is painted black. I repaired her nose. They were collecting money to have it repaired but I volunteered. Once I put that nose back on, I was a hero. The priest, Father Venus, had faith in me and would let me carry the collection plate sometimes. He used to say he was an "old white priest who had to talk to middle age Black women about marital problems." A couple of ladies with nothing else to do, would ask a lot of questions of Father Venus. I used to chime in and help him. They once asked him about Jesus having brothers, because it talked about Jesus and his brothers in the Bible.

"Those were stepbrothers," I told them. "As you can see from the Holy cards it was a second marriage."

Afterwards Father Venus said to me, "Thanks for helping me out, I hadn't thought of it myself." He always had confidence in me which gave me a boost.

There was a lady who went to a different church, a youth ministry at the Newman Center at USM, and I made friends with her. Her name was Sister Annette and she was the campus minister. She was a good friend to me and I used to help her out in the classes. The class was full of silly women, and you'd tell them things and they'd forget right away. The interesting thing is I should have been one of those students because I'm not a Catholic, not formally. I'm Church of England, Episcopalian, but I helped out anyhow. Mother went to church, but I think it was mainly because it was the proper and respectable thing to do. She went to the Episcopalian church next to the Lauren Rogers Museum. Like most mothers she'd say, "even though I can't see what you're up to, God does. You're never alone Mark!" For a long time when I was young I was nervous because I wondered if the guardian angels were watching.

Sister Annette would have been upset if she found out I wasn't Catholic, but I was helping with catechism classes. And this is one of my big personality flaws: I wouldn't even apply myself to become a proper Catholic. I didn't want to go through all that stuff, going to lessons and catechisms, and you can't just say you want to join. I would have converted but I didn't feel like going to all that trouble.

I used to give to St. Jude's Children's Hospital, way back when I couldn't afford it. Back in the 1990s they used to send you little square pictures of St. Jude's children. I used to give them $20 a month. When I got myself out of the group home I was so thankful that I donated money. I used to make checks out to a charity for hardly anything, and when the bank sent the checks back, I'd change it to a larger amount, maybe from $20 to $200, to impress Sister Annette, who was pleased. She had a lot of confidence in me. I was a show off even then. Everyone wants sometimes to impress people. I very much believe if something bothers your conscience it's a sin, but if it doesn't bother your conscience then it's not ... so let your conscience be your guide.

I thought about being a priest in high school, but I thought a seminary would be like being in jail. You can't play cards there. The group home was bad enough, so I know I wouldn't have liked the seminary. I may as well have gone to some of the lessons though. I don't want to be a priest and sit around in some place all day—one of those big grey depressing city churches in Chicago—for ten or twenty dollars and listen to old ladies complaining. I learned enough to make a convincing priest anyhow from watching "Father Brown." He was so compassionate and nice.

I'm like most people in that sometimes I am more religious on some days than others, depending on how I'm feeling. I do know I can't stand people who are staunch Christians, like televangelists, the type that will steal anything, who wear "GPS (gods plan for salvation)" T-shirts. I don't go to church now, and I usually have good excuses, which varies depending on who I'm talking to.

To supplement my income and have something to do I walked along Royal Street in New Orleans. Like on *Door to Door*, the film about the man with CP who wants to be a salesman. I remembered how nice they were to me at the New Orleans Museum of Art, so that's why I went to New Orleans to sell art. I would take a stack of 4 x 6 photos of my work and keep them in my pocket and go door to door. I carried my briefcase with a sample painting inside. I brought something appealing, like a girl with a cat. A lot of people like that sort of thing. The pastoral landscape Mother liked was always a winner, as well. I'd pull it out before they got mad at me going in—it's a salesmen's trick to catch their attention first. I had a winning picture, and before they could get mad and tell me to leave,

I'd show it to them. If they warmed up, I would ask to show my photographs. It's hard and it takes a lot of nerve.

This is how I met Josephine. She had a gallery on Royal Street in New Orleans. We just hit it off. She'd be so nice and charming to customers, but she could make a sailor blush with her language as soon as they left. As soon as someone else came into the gallery she would turn into a pleasant European lady. She and Mother got along all right on the phone. Josephine was a temperamental older lady, and she did enjoy taking advantage of tourists. We'd sell the same awful painting over and over again to people, New Orleans street scenes, and girls with cats. I also did holy cards to sell, not a lot of them but a few extra hundred helped me. Sometimes I'd use a holy card as my reference, and I'd do a bigger painting of it and sometimes improve it or add little things of my own.

She sold fake Faberge stuff and all kinds of things. I wasn't as good of a hack artist back then as I am now. She would sell tourists all kinds of things because she didn't really like them and she knew she'd never see them again, so it didn't matter.

I made up a phony resume that Josephine gave out sometimes at the gallery. I also used it or variations of it with other art galleries I managed to consign to. I lied on it about what I'd done in the 1980s and early 1990s. I said that I'd worked in advertising and animation, and that I was a member of a number or organizations like the National Watercolor Society and American Federation of Artists, the Pastoral Academy of this and that. I put down prestigious shows I'd been in.

I listed a number of galleries where I said I'd had exhibitions, like Ivory Kimpton Gallery in San Francisco, Galleria Veronese in New Orleans, and Gilman Gallery, Chicago. I decided to handwrite on the side of the page that I'd received an award from Mrs. Bush at the White House for donating a painting to the Committee for the Preservation of the White House. It was actually a real certificate they gave me, just a few months into the Bush administration. I gave them a 19th century watercolor of the White House by an unknown artist illustrator, supposedly done around 1870, something I'd actually painted myself. There is plenty of valuable anonymous art; look at folk art, you don't know who did it a lot of the time. I also gave them a James Sharples portrait of George Washington. When I gave the James Sharples they were going to have me meet Mrs. Bush but it was President Reagan's funeral, and a lot of stuff going on with important people from all over the world coming, so it just couldn't be done.

Josephine and I were good friends, soul mates really, because we'd joke we hoped buyers didn't look too closely at the picture until they were a long way away. Unlike Josephine I do try to please people nowadays and do my best.

Josephine had constant feuds with different businesses on the street, so of course I wouldn't sell anything at anyone else's gallery. There was another gallery interested and sold one of my paintings, but when Josephine found out she told me she wanted me to only sell for her, and of course I understood. It was extremely difficult to get money out of her though. The hardest part of being any kind of an artist is getting paid.

The last time I saw Josephine was 2007 and she died in 2008. Mother got a phone call from her son. She was an older woman, maybe around eighty. The last time I saw her she was still very much herself.

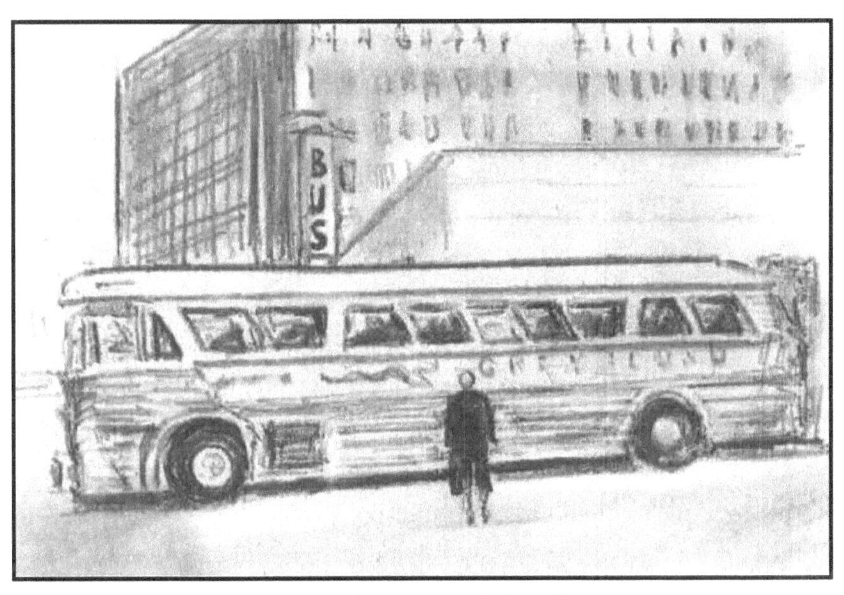

Illustration by Mark Landis

<u>**11**</u>

THE FORGERIES

I may have told many lies but I'm never untruthful. I think about the magician, The Amazing Randy, and his movie *An Honest Liar*. It's a good title. I didn't lie. I was misleading to people, using deceit and trickery, and not always saying a lie out loud. I'm an honest liar. At any rate, it's not a sin to lie; bearing false witness is.

I have a talent for arts and crafts … and forgeries. I have a bit of a savant in me. I donated my first picture to impress Mother, and to memorialize Dad. There was a good episode of "The Beverly Hillbillies"—my favorite one—where Mrs. Drysdale was endowing a museum and wanted it called after her or her father. She so reminded me of Mother that I decided to impress Mother with my donations.

Mother and I had a silent understanding about the philanthropy. I knew she knew, and she knew I knew she knew, but nothing was ever said. Occasionally, by her general demeanour, I could tell she liked something and she thought it was a good idea. She liked the letters from the bishop. Mother took me to the library in Hattiesburg where USM is, and they had a lot of art on display, and when I donated something I made sure there was a little plaque in memory of Dad, and I showed her. Mother was mad at me at the time because I didn't have any money and she had to go to a lot of trouble to get me disability, so naturally I was very happy that the philanthropy pleased her.

William H. Macy was so good in the movie *Door to Door,* and he looked a bit like me when I was fifty. I was impressed with that. The film begins with him polishing a pair of wing tips and I had a pair as well when I went on philanthropy trips. A lot of things in that movie resonated with me. People looked down on him, or just humoured him and I've had to put up with very similar problems. Our mothers weren't alike, only in that they both loved their sons.

When I was in the Menninger Clinic I wanted to be a commercial artist, maybe work for Hallmark Cards, and if I had gone to Kansas City maybe I could have worked there. But no one had confidence in me as commercial artist. Now, I wouldn't mind being called "a hack" because it at least means I'm competent. But I'd like to be better. I don't even know if I count as an artist, but I've improved a lot. Alex Stone wrote a book called *Fooling Houdini,* and he said that I kind of combine being a magician with being an artist.

Whenever there is an interview on art forgeries I talk about the Greenough family, who spent many years planning a remarkable forgery, where they conned a museum into paying a million dollars. The work of art was supposed to be a Gauguin statue of a satyr or a fawn, but it is ugly looking, something that someone in junior high could make. But the key is, the work of art isn't the statue. The work of art is something you never see. They forged a brilliant receipt of an art gallery in Paris in the 1900s, and so although, even if the receipt isn't something you see, I maintain that it's the *real* work of art.

The Greenough family had established a perfect provenance. That and the receipt, that's the true art. People pay a fortune for ugly looking things just because it's got enough paperwork or a good signature. I said that about some of the junk I did: It's the signature that must be right. The pictures I did weren't terrible; they were good enough if you didn't look too closely, but they were substandard compared to the real thing. It was no matter. I got the signatures right.

I've worked harder getting the paper to look old or making a frame from Goodwill look aged, than I've worked on the actual picture. When I'd travel and speak about my magnificent art collection, I'd cut frames out of catalogues and put it around a painting and make a *tromp l'oeil,* and I'd take a photo which I'd pull out of my pocket, showing it hanging by ancestral portraits. I was a magician. It was just about how things looked. Things are seldom what they seem.

I'd stopped donating paintings for a while, but then a lot of things happened right after Mother was gone because there was a flurry of activity. I was upset. That was a bad year for me. I went to an awful lot of places, which is why there are so many 'girl with a lute' paintings. Josephine died eight months before Mother so there was nowhere for me to sell my paintings and there was nothing for me to do. It wasn't like now. I had no friends at all. Josephine was gone, my friend Raymond had already died, and then Mother left me. I had nobody.

I like to draw and paint, but with nowhere to sell them, and being lonely and upset, I fell into philanthropy again and driving around in Mother's car all over the place. For many men, when they retire they still keep doing whatever they were doing. Two men at my friend Jacqueline's gallery keep working, like the retired shop teacher, so that's what I did, too. Even if there was no place for their work those men would probably still make the things they do, and I'm just like that. I'll sit around and make icons and just store them in Mother's bedroom.

There are a lot of misconceptions about how easy it was for me to donate my pictures. I recall an article where a museum official said that museums have to accept everything, particularly if it's donated by a wealthy collector they do not want to offend. Governments and politicians call this damage control. It's human nature to want to shift blame and avoid responsibility, but museums are notoriously closed and narrow in terms of what they want.

Museums should have a direction and a mission and collect relevant things, which is what they do. They have acquisition boards. Think in terms of very exclusive condominiums in New York or a club; not everyone can get in. Museums can be quite stuffy and that's why you need to know what they collect. When you read about scandals you can't help but wonder how people are so gullible, and you ask yourself why they were never suspicious. But people *are* initially suspicious. Yet, once they are convinced of the *first* thing, everything else is easy to believe. It's psychological. We're all like that, and museums are like this too.

As far as I'm concerned, once you convince someone about the origin of the painting or the artist, they'll take anything no matter how bad it is. They say that in making your first million, making the first hundred thousand dollars is the most difficult and the rest is easy. I've found convincing someone to accept a forgery to be similar. It's hardest at the beginning. One thing I found to be true: If somebody is any good at being a spy or a con man, you wouldn't suspect them. That's the whole point. It's not like with James Bond where he looks like a spy. If a liar is any good at all you don't even start to suspect them.

Everybody makes mistakes, and it's fair that museums make mistakes. I've been in a lot of storage rooms, which all museums have because they rotate their exhibits, or they take things down to storage if there is an attribution problem, which is common. When I was at the Savannah School they'd pull out things to see what I thought, and ask my opinions on things, like if they'd misattributed works to the wrong artists.

I remember being shown an early 18th century Scottish artist, Sir William Beechey, who was a portrait artist, a Romney or Sir Edward Lawrence-type person. The curator showed me a portrait of two young boys and asked if I thought it was done by Sir William Beechey and I remember saying, "This boy here, his face is really good, it's great, a masterpiece… the other boy's face is competent…"

I said that nobody is consistent; it's like in professional sports, sometimes athletes are doing well and sometimes they are off, and artists are no different so the portrait could well be his and they could probably attribute it to him. After the Sir William Beechey painting there was another painting they showed me, a big old landscape painting. I noticed things some other people hadn't.

I was in a museum once, perhaps the Nelson Atkins, although I'm not entirely sure, and they were commenting that it was very unusual that on the only northern European painting they had the Virgin had a halo. Usually, you don't see that in Flemish paintings. But I had a story for everything. I already knew about churches imposing penance and I also knew the Duchess of Burgundy had an artist illustrating her for her book.

She drove the artist to commit a murder, a very Medieval type thing. His penance was given to him by the priest, as they often were in those days, and he was told to go on a pilgrimage that delayed the Duchess's book being done by quite a bit; maybe it was never even finished.

I already knew about all that, and what I did was embellish it. In the late Middle Ages painters were considered craftsmen and weren't lofty like they are now. They didn't start to get pretentious until the Renaissance. I told the museum staff that on the artist's way on the pilgrimage, which took a long time because it was the Middle Ages, making it dangerous and expensive, he had to stop off at different monasteries to prove he'd been on the pilgrimage. I added that, naturally, he'd want to see what others of his craft were doing. He went to Italy and saw the halos and came back and did his own religious paintings and put in a halo and then some others took it up. I made it all up.

A lot of those artists whose work I donated don't even exist. I had a lot of good-looking medieval-type frames I was able to bang up, and they needed pictures. If I had done an academic picture to put in the frames I would just make up a name and a birth and death date. There were an awful lot of academic artists between 1500 and 1900 that even experts, people with degrees in art, have never heard of. They'd have to go to their big reference book, or it would take some searching to learn about them. And there were lots of good, competent artists it took a while to discover. Take Vermeer; he'd been forgotten and then was rediscovered. They are always rediscovering artists as others go out of fashion.

In terms of the way I used to do things, I had a box of old catalogues left over from San Francisco, and I used a catalogue description, because a lot of times the catalogues from the early 1970s and 1980s didn't have an illustration for everything. I remember looking through a catalogue and reading about nymphs sitting on rocks and thinking, *that looks promising*, and so I came up with a nymph that would have looked like Everett Shinn did it. Early on, some of the things I painted may have seemed kind of strange, but I was limited to my collection of art catalogues from Sotheby's, Christie's and Phillip's. I got to be good at Paul Signac. They fell for them right away. Every time I thought I might take a trip I'd go to the library first. The public library had a fairly good art section and I'd Xerox pages to be used like catalogue references.

While visiting museums I'd show up with copies and say they were from an auction catalogue, and I'd tell them I couldn't bring the real catalogues because I needed them as I had other things from that auction. Before the Internet, when deciding what to donate all I had to go on was a great big green reference book, *The Directory of U.S. Museums and Living Displays*, and it would list every museum by state. When it described collections it would give a comprehensive explanation of what they'd collect. I was the only person who ever used that book, the nosy librarian told me.

Back in 2010 I was able to search the collection to see what they wanted, but when I first started in the 1990s I had no idea what individual museums collected. Once or twice I'd offer something really valuable, and they wouldn't want it because they only collected certain time periods or regional art. Sometimes the directory would say 18th to 19th century art, but that covers a lot and didn't give me much to go by, so I wouldn't really know exactly what they'd take and I'd have to guess. Even when I brought something a museum should have wanted, sometimes a curator didn't want it or even know about it, although you'd expect him to be familiar with his museum's whole collection and artists who are relevant.

A couple of times a curator would say, "That's not my speciality," but it should have been something they at least understood. I know education is specialized now, but I was taken aback. I'd think, *you don't know much and you're a curator ... you have a degree from Harvard ...* I remember I'd go to the ones in Texas where they'd mostly collect Western Art, but it was more than once I'd be with the curator and I'd have a cowboy picture like a Borein or a Remington, and nobody had heard of them. How could they not know who Edward Borein is? He was one of the most popular painters of Western scenes in America in the 1920s. But the curators wouldn't know him and would say something like, "My speciality is 18th century French art." Seems like somebody wouldn't be very good at their job if they have a narrow focus on what they know. I've never had a responsible job, but if I'd worked for a museum it seems it would be part of my job to know about these things.

Donating forgeries is kind of an adventure. I was able to make people think I was a multi-millionaire even though I was riding buses. I only went back and forth to certain museums, and others I only went to once. I changed my name each time, but it was over a period of thirty years, starting when I was being a benefactor to first impress Mother. I remember telling at least one director of a gallery in New Orleans three different names and he never did recognize me.

The one visit in the middle wouldn't count because I dealt with the chief curator and the director wasn't even there. It was a bit exciting because I took a chance he'd recognize me. I'd often pretend to be from the family of the founders of the museum in Laurel. Museum directors meet so many people that when I suggested we'd met before he thought we had. I liked him best. I did a very nice Zachary Taylor plate from 1849 for the museum in New Orleans.

It was easiest for me to go to museums that weren't too far away. I often went to the Jackson Museum of Art. I went too many times because it was easy to get to; I could just get to it on the bus. If I'd lived in New York, for example, I would have gone to other ones. I started closest to where I lived and then went outwards. From the group home in Hattiesburg until I came to live with Mother, I always kept my address in Laurel because I thought it was better for a wealthy philanthropist. I'd associate myself with the art gallery here. I'd keep a mail drop in Michigan and New Orleans, through Mailboxes Etc. and then they'd forward it.

I used a number of different names through the years. It was just practicality and nothing devious that made me use the name James Brantley for philanthropy, my stepfather's name. All Mother's accounts were in my stepfather's name and there's an old saw 'if it's not broken don't fix it.' I've tried to get the Internet company to get things changed to my name, but even with the death certificate of my mother they don't change it; they just keep it in his name just as they did for Mother, so I use his email address.

I tended to look for new names in catalogues. I noticed provenances of paintings in the possession of certain families and Scott was one, so I used the name Arthur Scott. I also used the name Stephen Gardiner with visiting museum officials to the Lauren Rogers. There are so many Gardiners in Laurel, and the Gardiner family founded the Lauren Rogers Museum. They weren't mad at all when they found out and they have since taken me up and been quite good to me. They were friends of Bunny Wyndham, and I painted their children and grandchildren, and if there is a big event at their house they invite me.

In New Orleans I met George Rodrigue who did the famous "blue dog" paintings. He used to show up at events and the director used to introduce me as Steven Gardiner, an important patron. I talked to him, and both he and his wife were quite pleasant. Other names I used were Marc Lanois, Stephen Grau, Stephen Grey, Stephen Grauman, and Mark Linsey. Mother didn't mind if I changed my name from time to time. She saw the letters and knew I was changing my name and was just glad I got my father's name right.

When people were meeting me at airports I would say, "I'm an unimpressive little old bald man in a green suit." My personality depended on who I was with. You wouldn't expect someone with million-dollar paintings to live in a housing project. When I got into Federation Towers, when curators came they probably thought I was eccentric, living in a housing project and giving away paintings worth a hundred thousand dollars. Someone from the University of Mississippi drove up to see me to get their pictures. I've loved spy stories and intrigue my whole life.

My life was not as extreme as the movie *Catch Me if You Can*, but there were times I used to think, *look at me—I'm living a double life!* When I was twenty-two and I came back from a bus trip I showed my first caseworker at the housing project the certificate from my endowed gift to a museum. Heaven only knows what she thought I was doing with that;

she must have thought I was having delusions of grandeur. They must get used to people telling them all manner crazy things.

No one noticed I was a would-be artist because I didn't tell anyone. My friend Raymond kind of knew I could draw because occasionally I'd be describing something and I might sketch it out. But no one at the nursing home knew anything about me, and no one knew about my secret life. Like in movies about sleeper agents, where characters may appear to be the typical family next door, but really they are agents, I quietly led a double life.

I never donated anything too big. I didn't have the nerve to show up with something worth millions in my briefcase. I'm not that talented an actor. I kept it realistic. I liked to do paintings under $50,000 because they were small and I could put them in my briefcase. When I travelled on the bus, which was a good deal of time, or on a plane, I only took smaller pieces. I had a black travelling bag, two or three of them since 1989, and I could fit my paintings inside.

I've never checked bags on planes and always like to have everything with me, so the painting went in the cabin with me. Once Mother started letting me use the car and I could drive places that's when I started giving away bigger pieces, like Girl with a Lute. I could just put them in the backseat. I was never worried at a museum or school, I could slip right into my act, because I'd used up my anxiety getting to those places. The stuff I was worried about was the challenges of actually getting to museums, dealing with people in bus stations, finding places with no maps, having very little money.

Those were my biggest challenges. I never worried when I was in a museum and around people and pretending to be a benefactor, but I was scared on the trip there. In the early 2000s and I drove through Atlanta it was very stressful. Once or twice I rented a car to go to places like Louisiana. Later I used Mother's car when I inherited it.

I have good color judgement. Before the internet and when I got a computer in 2005, I relied on my catalogues which were black and white, but I was still able to produce a good color painting. About twelve years ago, I guess there was gossip and some people were getting suspicious. Paintings have provenances and so they've been published sometimes. An old book will make a photo look different than a book printed now, or even books printed by different companies will make art appear different. I once went into a big museum, and they took me into a boardroom, and they had every book sitting there with photos, which made me quite nervous. I'd done the painting I was giving them from an old catalogue from the 1960s which was black and white, and I'd added my own color. I didn't have access to anything that would have told me which colors to use.

My heart was thumping, and I thought, *how am I going to talk my way out of this one*? It seemed like they had ten books with the same picture in it and the colors varied a little, but it turned out I had guessed the colors right. They looked at my picture under a magnifying glass and my colors matched. I was impressed with myself. There was a bit of a variation in my own work, but it made sense. Everything was terrific after that. As far as things I did for museums none of them were particularly difficult. Naturally some pieces took longer than others.

When I first started philanthropy The Palace of the Legion of Honour gave me a good book of their collections and then I got addicted to collecting art books. Museums would let me loose in their gift shops, so I'd load up. I'm like King Midas when it comes to art books and I can't get enough of them. I needed them for reference and to have illustrations to copy or refer to.

Once I told the museum staff I'd fallen asleep in the airport in Oklahoma City and when I'd awoken someone had stolen my art books, so I got to loot the gift shop a second time. Nobody had actually stolen them. I'd sent everything by FedEx from the hotel.

 Often when I was donating artwork I dressed as a Jesuit priest. People would come up to touch me for luck, just touch my shoulder. The Jesuits use casuistry, a way of justifying everything—the ends justify the means. A good Jesuit Father could convince you of things.

If I'd been a priest I would have been a nice one, not one that frightened people. Sometimes priests complain about listening to people, but they're humans, too. They can't always tell how many people show up for communion and the holy wine has to be consumed, and the reason some of them become drunks is because they finish it up, so it doesn't go to waste. I would have been a good priest; I had a lot of reassuring references from the bible, and I would give these passages to people.

Corinthians 12:3 and 4 was a common one. *And I know such a man— whether in the body or out of the body I do not know, God knows—How he was caught up into Paradise and heard inexpressible words, which it is not lawful for a man to utter.* I didn't have the discipline to become a priest though. I don't know how my parents would have felt if I had become one; Mother probably wouldn't have minded.

I get on these mailing lists and there's a service you can subscribe to, and they'll write sermons for busy priests, although they can be changed if need be. I've never had a priest as a great friend who would share a secret like that, and tell me if they bought their sermons, and perhaps that would be like your darkest secret as a priest and no one would admit to it anyway.

There was a short-lived TV series of named "The Bells of St Mary's" in the early 1960s. Gene Kelly played the priest and helped his parishioners with family-related problems. I used to take buses all over being a philanthropist, and when you spend all sorts of time at the bus station you see the dregs of society. They trusted me because I was a priest.

Invariably, if you're dressed as a priest in an airport or bus station somebody is going to come up to you. I was at a bus stop in Jackson on my way to an art museum called the Dixon Museum, and there was a Mexican family who had everything in the world tied up in boxes with them. They couldn't really speak English, but the young man made it understood they needed to go do something and have me watch their things. They were a nice young family with very small children, and I gestured I could watch their possessions. It probably seemed longer than it was, but I paced around and stood guard over it for ages. They came back and they were extremely grateful, and I blessed them, and they got on their bus and left.

After a while I was worried there'd be a lot of gossip about someone memorializing their mother, so I invented a sister. It doesn't make sense, but if I thought logically and consistently then I wouldn't have gotten myself into a mess in the first place. People say, "Let's cross that bridge when we get to it," but instead I always think, *let's cross the river when we get to a bridge*. That's kind of how I went about things; I worried about everything after the fact. One of the reasons I chose the name Emily for my sister is because it's a name you remember. I watched a play, *Our Town,* when it was made into a film. We'd had to read it in high school or college. Sometimes I'd read the whole book because there wasn't anything else to do in class. Emily is a character in it, which is one of the reasons it's a reassuring name for me, and that's why I ended up using it.

The movie version of *Our Town* made an impression on me as well, because like for all teenage boys, there was a pretty actress in the role of Emily. Glynnis O'Connor is another actress who played Emily. I'd see her in an after school special, or one thing or another, although not as much as I'd see other pretty actresses, like Joanne Harris and Darlene Carr. They were in things I'd see from time to time in the 1980s, but in the 1970s I saw them a lot. Darlene Carr was in all sorts of different shows. Joanne had more range as an actress; she played a bad girl on many shows, but she played a good girl too, and even a detective.

When I'd go to the Brooks in Memphis, I made friends with people at the Memphis College of Art, and I'd prolong things and come up with excuses to go there. I gave them a Signac and a little miniature on copper of Cephalous, from Greek mythology. I did everything I could to find excuses to go up there to the Brooks as a benefactor. I used to like to sit around and talk to the students and I made friends with them. I hated to say I got lonely, but I did, and loneliness is the root of why I donated pictures to them. I was really down when I knew it was the last visit. They were going to build some sort of addition to the college, and I had said I'd give money for the addition. You can get carried away in certain situations, and on that occasion I'd gotten really carried away. They were supposed to come get my art collection, so I had to just disappear. I felt real down thinking, *Gee, that's the last time I'm going to see people like Erin and the other students*. It made me quite depressed.

I went to other schools to meet art students, but it never was the same. Most other schools were far away so I used to just go there once and stay a few days. There is always someone at these schools who learned art in Europe. There was someone impressed by my academic nymph, and I believe it was on the poster for my show later in life. I met nice students at the Savannah College of Art. They had one of those big old houses for important visitors. It's a beautiful school and I very much enjoyed the visit, but I never met students I liked as much as I did in Memphis.

That's why I got into children's books. The University of Southern Mississippi has the de Grummond Collection, the best collection of children's literature in our hemisphere. I had to find something to do for illustrations to bring to their collections. In order to give them illustration art I needed to get books to copy so I started collecting children's books. I did *Tales of Uncle Remus with pictures of* Brer Rabbit and Brer Fox. I would find a book at Goodwill, which with an inscription it would be worth thousands, and I'd show up with things like that from time to time.

I did a Charles Schulz with an inscription: *To Mother, Jo.* I did lots of stuff for them like Dr. Seuss, Charles Schulz, and Maurice Sendak, things that are easy to do. I remember one time there was a reproduction children's book I gave that would have been extremely valuable if it had been real; I think it was one of the first Hardy Boys book, *Footprints Under the Window.* I found it at Books a Million, on a little table at the front where they get rid of books, and it was only a dollar. There wasn't anything I could do about the cover, but I was able to bang up the book really well and disguise other things that were giveaways, and I made it look exactly like a first addition. I had a wonderful time doing it too. Then I transformed it as though a little boy in the 1940s, perhaps around age seven or eight, had got at it with his pencils. I put all kinds of things on it, like World War II airplanes shooting down the Japanese. Even like that the book would be valuable and they really liked it at the de Grummond. They were always nice to me.

I would usually stay a while because they had students there working and I'd like to sit around and talk to them, which they'd do because I was a rich philanthropist. They had to be nice to me and take an interest in me. Sometimes we'd talk about literature, art, and TV shows for a couple of hours. I hated it when I had to quit going. They're done with me now.

I remember the curator at the Lauren Rogers was real rude to me once because it was a rainy day, and she reprimanded me for bringing a wet umbrella into a room. I was with two curators who'd come to collect a picture from me and I acted a bit like I owned the gallery. I didn't always feel like travelling and sometimes curators went to the Lauren Rogers to pick up other paintings, so I could meet them all there at the same time.

When she left the room, I showed them how she talked to me, and they sympathized with me and didn't blame me. I then told them I wanted to favor other museums, that I'd chosen their museum for my own reasons, and I didn't want the Lauren Rogers to know about it, or my family. Because she had been rude to me they understood why I was withdrawing my favor from the Lauren Rogers.

Way back The Lauren Rogers Museum of Art in Laurel was friendly to me because I was a philanthropist and benefactor. I gave them Nymph on a Rock by Everett Shinn. I got off the bus with my bag at Lauren Rodgers and they didn't even know I lived here.

My connection with Mrs. Hall is probably one of the reasons I got in trouble with the Lauren Rogers Museum. People in Hattiesburg may have known I did art. Mrs. Patty Hall was in charge of a thing called the Arts Council, which was in an old Carnegie library, although they eventually moved into a new building.

I was a terrible artist when she first met me, but I could hack out a few things like landscapes which she would sell from time to time. She didn't know about the philanthropy, only that I was an artist. She had a lot of paintings by me, including a big Presbyterian church I painted. She and Mother were friends of a sort, and whenever there was a fundraiser or charity auction they would invariably have me do a painting for it.

Mother had me do the same thing over and over, whatever was popular—girl with a cat or English country landscapes; I just turned those things out whenever there was any kind of charity thing. One of those ended up at a Lauren Rodgers fundraiser of some sort. I should have known better, but maybe Mrs. Hall didn't tell me it was going to be at the museum. The Lauren Rogers Museum is still implacably mad at me. Everyone around here used to try to use their influence on them so I could go back, but they are still mad and will never forgive me.

When I went to the Oklahoma City Museum of Art, the chief curator drove me around and I spent a lot of time with him. He was an old man at that time and gone now, but I'd recognize him again if I saw him. I never really spent time with Matt Leininger, the registrar, the one who figured out what I was doing with my philanthropy and decided to stop me. It's sort of an interesting parallel of why I had to leave Chicago, when that friend got mad that I'd forged staff IDs and so he'd made it hard for me. I'd completely forgotten Matt Leininger, and so when I met him again after he'd discovered my ruse, I didn't recognize him. We got along though.

Aside from a few close calls, fortunately, I never got caught when I was actually out making a donation. I could tell a curator or some underling or subordinate was suspicious but they didn't dare say anything to the museum director who is the dictator—always powerful and everyone kowtows to them. You don't contradict Mr. Big. I remember a few times that happened.

Sometimes I did find out later that I was in trouble. I remember one time they must have found out the next day, but I was long gone. I'd get one of those stiff letters saying they needed to return the picture. Some museums were actually nice about sending the paintings back. I didn't usually open them when I received them—I was afraid to. Because I used the mailboxes at Mailboxes Etc., probably lots of things were sent back but I'd close up the mailbox after a while and move on.

I kind of thought I'd be giving away paintings for the rest of my life. I should have been suspicious people were talking about me. I got the impression the bishops were talking together and noticing that someone was going around giving them icons. I don't know what I'd have said if I'd been caught. I would have thought of something. I would have said that I was duped or something.

At one point The Financial Times kept showing up on call display on my phone and I just ignored it. Maybe the caller left messages, but the machine was in Mother's room and might have been full anyhow, so if there were any left I never knew. It was driving me crazy how often they called but it didn't occur to me that they'd want to speak to me, because Mother was the one who subscribed to things. Not that she read them. She'd get Fortune, but the issues just sat there. I looked at them. And so I thought the calls had to do with either her subscription or Mother's account at Edward Jones, where her stock market stuff was. People magazine called too but Mother got that one as well and so it all seemed to me to be subscription drives.

I used to check Wikipedia for Laurel to read about notable residents, and for a long time it listed me as a notable person, as a retired art dealer and philanthropist for donating art. I didn't check it all that often, just every once in a while. Mother was gone at this point. I checked sometime in 2011, and was very much surprised to see that instead of calling me a "retired art dealer" it had a reference to an article in the Guardian, which is a UK paper, so I read it and I must say, it came as a shock. It had a great deal of negative things about me. It said I was a "crook" and like along the lines of, "his game is up".

This should have tipped me off about why the Financial Times was really calling, but it didn't. A little while later, on a Thursday or Friday, John Gapper, a writer for The Times, showed up. I heard banging on the door but didn't answer it. He was still out at midnight calling and standing in the cold because he saw a light on. I started thinking that maybe The Financial Times was calling for the same reason the Guardian did an article about me, and so I called John the next day, just to see what it was about, and he was pleased to talk. We are almost the same age. He came to visit practically the next day.

He was worried before he arrived and wanted to make sure I was there. I don't blame him; I'd put him through a lot. He asked questions in a cautious way. When I first met him and he sat down, I said, "So I've been stopped, huh?" and he thought it was funny. We spent the day together. I was still afraid of getting into trouble, so I showed him my mental health stuff, like the Menninger Foundation paperwork, and especially the good stuff, like my IQ results. Mother would have liked that. He asked me not to speak to anybody until his article came out, which I didn't, and he's been a friend to me ever since.

People often say I was doing performance art. Maybe it's true, but I didn't know it if I was. If I had thought I was a performance artist I wouldn't have been performing. And certainly sticking it to the art world never occurred to me.

At no point did I ever sell one of my forgeries or accept a tax receipt. For me, it never started for money, and it never became about that. It was the same in 1986 as it was all the way through. I've been in mental institutions and group homes, but haven't been in jail, and frankly, those were bad enough. From what I've heard and read about it, jail is awful. Some of the guys in the group home had been in jail and they'd talk about it. I've also read about it on Quora. Even before the COVID pandemic, people in prison were constantly sick because of crowding, and I can't imagine being in an awful prison and then having a cold. Maybe if I hadn't had those experiences in group homes and hospitals I would have risked more. Usually, art forgers have partners in the art business like a crooked dealer who had fashionable contacts, usually a bunch of people in league, and their stories are more complicated than mine.

Way back, when I went into that very first museum, if they'd just said "thanks a lot" I might not have done it again, but everyone was so nice and I'd never been treated like that before. Before that happened I had never been treated like royalty. It sometimes infuriates me when celebrities complain about attention; I imagine they'd yell in protest if it stopped. I certainly got addicted to it. No one ever respected me until the first time I donated a picture to a museum.

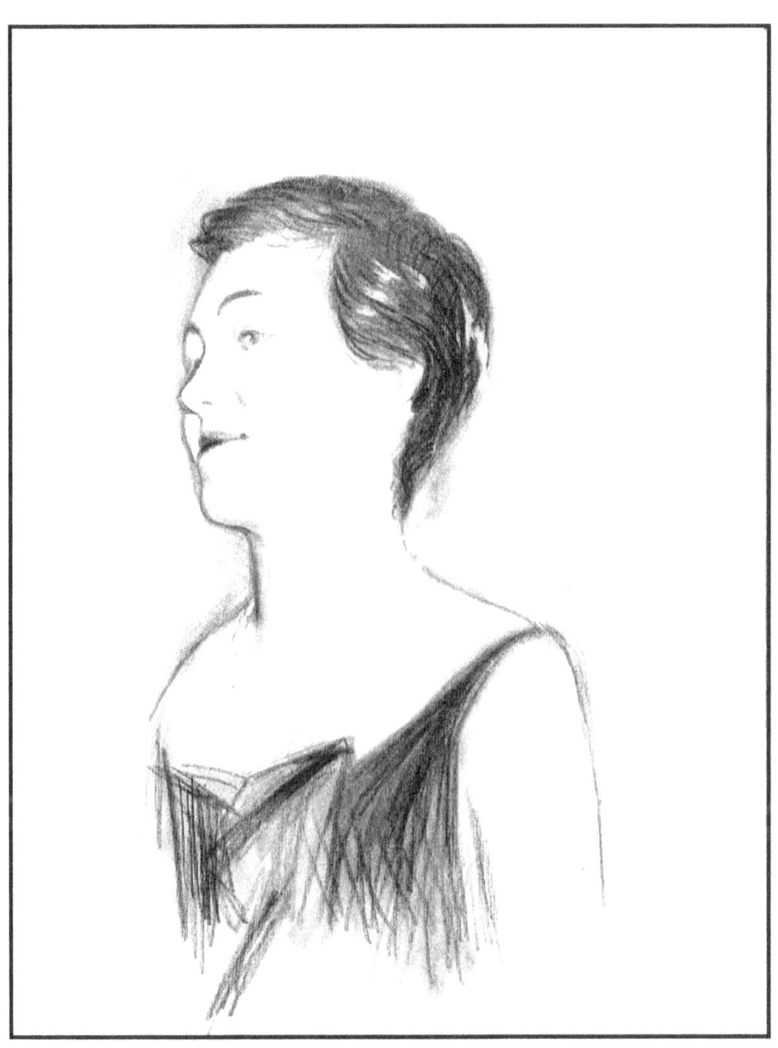

Illustration by Mark Landis

<u>12</u>

MOTHER

I always called her "Mother" because Dad didn't approve of the term Mom. People have all sorts of humor about all sorts of things, but they have no of sense of humor about their mother. Everybody is very, very sensitive. You can't say anything about family. Even so, I imagine that if I were to make a movie about Mother it would be like a situation comedy. The camera would show her in a big aristocratic palace, a place like in *The Swan* starring Grace Kelly, and then there would be a fade out and you'd see something from a *Ma and Pa Kettle* movie.

That's going a bit far, but it always impressed me that Mother could completely ignore the way it really was sometimes. She was always worried about decorum and dignity and whether something looked right. That's why I'm always worried about how things look. In everything she said or did, she had to think if one of the upper class would agree. Real rich people don't think like that.

At St. Mary's School in London we went on field trips, and went to one or two stately homes, where they would have classical paintings, as well as the museum in London. Someone warned us boys to behave ourselves because there may be paintings that might get us into trouble, classical paintings, mythical things, nymphs, Apollo and Daphne—all of which might have some nudity which could get boys snickering.

But Mother had taught me that it was art. She was very definite about that. Like a lot of people she was inconsistent about things. If some nudity showed up in a movie she'd go into hysterics. One time when I took her to a hospital in Jackson, we were in a hotel room and she said, "Mark you can watch TV." She practically made me. I turned to channels I didn't get. Movies are more realistic nowadays and there was a bad word and she got so upset. I told her it wasn't my fault and I'd turn it off, but that didn't

134

help. Now I can't psychologically say those words because of her. Nothing could ever cause me to say a bad word, it's just constitutionally impossible because of Mother's reaction to swear words.

In 2005 Hurricane Katrina forced me to leave Hattiesburg and move back in with Mother. It wasn't really bad there where she lived, but bad enough, with no power or water for about a week. Finally, I got in touch with Mother and she had a friend drive her to come and get me. I ended up living with her a little less than five years. I didn't have much stuff when I left Hattiesburg. She hired someone with a pickup truck to go get the last things I left behind a couple of weeks later. There were no storage lockers because they were full at the time with so many people in a similar position leaving their homes. We filled up the storage room upstairs in Mother's building instead and I threw away a lot of things.

While I was at home with Mother after the hurricane she became dependent on me. It was a sign I should stay with her; she was getting on in years and there were things I could do for her, and I think it made it easy on her for a little while. I did a lot of things to make things easier on her, essentially anything she told me to do. Mother wouldn't let me drive, however, because she didn't trust me.

She was one of those mothers who treat their sons like they're ten years old their entire lives. Dad hadn't taught me to drive because he died and Mother was so uptight, it was simply beyond her; but eventually she needed me to drive her appointments. That was the worst thing I ever had to tell her, that with old age she had too many tickets and too many accidents and so they wouldn't renew her insurance. I didn't tell her right away. I told her I was still looking into it. Eventually I had to and that's when I took over at the wheel.

The last year or two she wasn't really the same, after she had neurosurgery. In some ways she was nicer and in some was she was more irritable. One thing I noticed was that Mother wasn't quite as suspicious or alert as she used to be. Five years before, Mother would have found out I'd started to drink, but at this point she didn't notice I was drinking.

My aunt lived with us when I moved back after the hurricane. Mother supported her but appreciated the companionship. They stayed in their room and I stayed in mine and we would only see each other doing business. Sometimes we would talk but not for long. We never had any real conversations. Ours were mostly business type conversations or if she was mad at me. I often complained about her relatives, and sometimes she agreed and sometimes she didn't. Even after my aunt left, Mother and I still didn't do a lot together. We just ate meals on trays in our rooms. The last time I remember the family sitting down together for a meal was in the 1960s when Dad was alive.

Mother had all the Julia Child cookbooks. She didn't cook Southern foods; she made French things. I remember her making crepes a few times. Not long ago I put one of Mother's recipes in a cookbook for the home renovation show "Home Town," with Erin and Ben Napier. It featured recipes from people in Laurel. They said I was one of the greatest art forgers of the 20th century. I contributed Boeuf Bourguignon en Cocotte on page 34. I picked the recipe because it wasn't real long and complicated, and Mother would have approved. I did an illustration for the book as well.

Although Mother did cook she didn't do it all the time, and when she started to go downhill she would send me out for food. Mother would send me out to restaurants she approved of. Laurel wasn't the way it is now and didn't have as big a selection.

Between the hurricane and the end, she was always getting mad at me about one thing or another. She had boxes and boxes of receipts and records. She was paranoid that her identity might be stolen because of commercials she saw on TV. Mother had a big industrial shredder. She told me to shred everything, boxes and boxes worth of paperwork, and I said I would do it while she was out playing bridge. She had a big social life and she was gone a fair bit. I just bagged it up and threw it away. When she asked me about it, I said that I had shredded it, but she didn't believe me. Somehow Mother knew I hadn't done it. You can't hide things from mothers; they always know what's going on. She'd often say, "I hope you're happy someone will steal my identity when I die." But I couldn't possibly have shredded that amount; it would have taken weeks and it was full of staples.

She was always exasperated by things like my lying. She'd say, "Mark, I promise I won't get mad if you tell me the truth." Unfortunately, mothers will say they won't get angry if they're told the truth, but they're campaign promises—empty promises. When I was ten years old she'd ask for the truth, but then go back on her promise and I got in trouble anyway. I don't remember what I'd done, but I do remember I never fell for those promises again. I would never, ever trust her again and I'd deny anything right to the end. She would let me get away with things sometimes. We were both kind of soulmates, inclined to mischief.

I could ask her for money if she was in a good mood, but it was hard to get money from her. You had to hint and be subtle. Mother had no ability with money. Like on "I Love Lucy," Mother would shop to feel better. She bought an expensive red Cadillac after Dad died. She was seventy-eight years old. Mother was bitter towards Dad at the end. More than a few times she'd complain, "Mark your father left us nothing." She threw personal letters out and I'm not sure if that had anything to do with it.

Mother knew what was going on with the forgeries. We had a ton of locks but then we got a burglar alarm and we didn't need it. Mother would always forget the code and she'd have the police there. She'd get up at 4:00 A.M. to let me out of the apartment when I was going to give paintings and she'd give me a look. She would get nice letters from cardinals and archbishops for my icon donations in Dad's memory. She did specifically tell me she was pleased when she would get something from a bishop. But I could already kind of tell she was pleased just by her expression, there would be kind of a subtle smile. Usually, she never said anything to me. She was like that. Anyone can light a candle in church, so my philanthropy mattered more. Mother's bathroom has icons stacked up to the rafters. Giving them away to churches isn't the same without Mother here and getting the letters doesn't feel the same.

I was always trying to get into favor with Mother. After I was living with her I went back to visit San Francisco. I was going to go to the modern art museum but I spent so much time at the Legion of Honour Museum that I came home. I decided to use up some of my credit card while I was there. I used to go by Shrieve and Company on Post Street downtown, a prestigious store, and one day I went in and bought a Hermes watch for Mother. It cost almost $4,000 in 2007. She was real pleased and she'd wear it all the time. I'd ask her to be careful with it which would irritate her. Mother had a lot of jewellery, lots of cloisonné. She had a fleur de lis with little turquoise stones that was Grandmother's.

When Mother was sick I maxed out all my credit cards buying her things like jewellery, but she didn't have much chance to wear it. I just wanted to spend money on her. It's difficult to change when you're older. After Mother left, I was upset and I went on a spending binge and ruined my credit cards. I also went to museums as far away as Kansas City. I ordered a lot of room service, too. They took away my American Express. When I inherited money I bought a lot of shoes online, but they were sales on overstock, and some didn't even fit and others fell apart. I got top of the line shoes for the Rockefeller show. It's the kind of thing old people talk about it.

My aunt and her family took advantage of Mother. I heard my aunt and cousin laughing over the phone at Mother one day, about her eccentricities, about her ways. I tried to tell Mother about it, but if she didn't want to hear something she didn't hear it, and it took some time before she believed me. Mother had lent them a fortune for their business which was failing. I'd have twice as much money as I do now if Mother hadn't given them so much, although what would I have done with more money? I'm most bitter about them trying to take Mother's jewelry, which is why I had to hide it. Mother didn't need expensive jewelry in the hospital like they claimed. I brought it out again after my aunt died.

Mother had been going downhill for a long time, and I was pacing around frequently. She had all kinds of problems at that point. I would go on day trips and people would look in on her. I used to take her to the doctor—that was one of my jobs. We'd go to Jackson, Mississippi. One day she was getting dressed to go to the doctor's, but didn't come out of her room. I knocked but there was no reply. I opened door and found she'd collapsed. I didn't call the ambulance because she was sort of talking. Mother had gained a lot of weight so I couldn't lift her. She'd knocked over a table and lamp and I guess it made a lot of noise because someone else in the building showed up and called the ambulance and it escalated from there. She went to emergency, lost consciousness, and never regained it. It never occurred to me I wouldn't be with her in the future. I thought we'd always be together. So now I don't think of the future because it comes too fast.

Mrs. Hall is one person I wouldn't want to see again, even though I always liked her, because she took me to the hospital when Mother was in critical care, and she was with me when the surgeon came to talk to me. They didn't take you to a special waiting room back then to tell you bad news. I remember seeing my friend Raymond in hospital in the early 1990s and I was going through one of those general waiting rooms.

There was a middle-aged man who had just received some terrible news and he just completely lost control of himself and started crying uncontrollably, and I remember thinking at the time, that's awful, to have to do that in a public waiting room. I had hoped if that ever happened to me I'd be able to get a better grip on myself.

But when the surgeon came and told me Mother had died I just lost complete control and started crying. I made such a scene! When you let yourself go in front of somebody you don't want to see them again. I haven't seen Mrs. Hall since that day. I didn't get as upset when Dad died. I've never experienced anything like the reaction I had over Mother. If my life had depended on it, I couldn't have controlled myself. Sometimes I wonder if that man I saw back in the 1990s had just lost a parent.

I don't think about Dad as much as I do about Mother because I didn't know him as well. After she was gone and I went through her belongings I found all kinds of things. That's when I found the check from someone who hadn't paid me. It was $500 and it had just sat there.

Mother didn't read mysteries like Dad did. Mother got books at W. H. Smith Stationer, mainly in the UK and Europe. She read Danielle Steele and the sort of thing you'd expect, and I gave them away after she was gone. The things I liked I kept. Going through her things I saw she saved drawings I did back in junior high. It choked me up when I saw that, and it brought a tear to my eye.

I have nothing unresolved with Mother. Things were always just kind of the same. She always treated me like a ten-year-old and we always understood each other. I wouldn't want to change our relationship because it would be strange. It's just how we were. For it to be different she would have to have been somebody else.

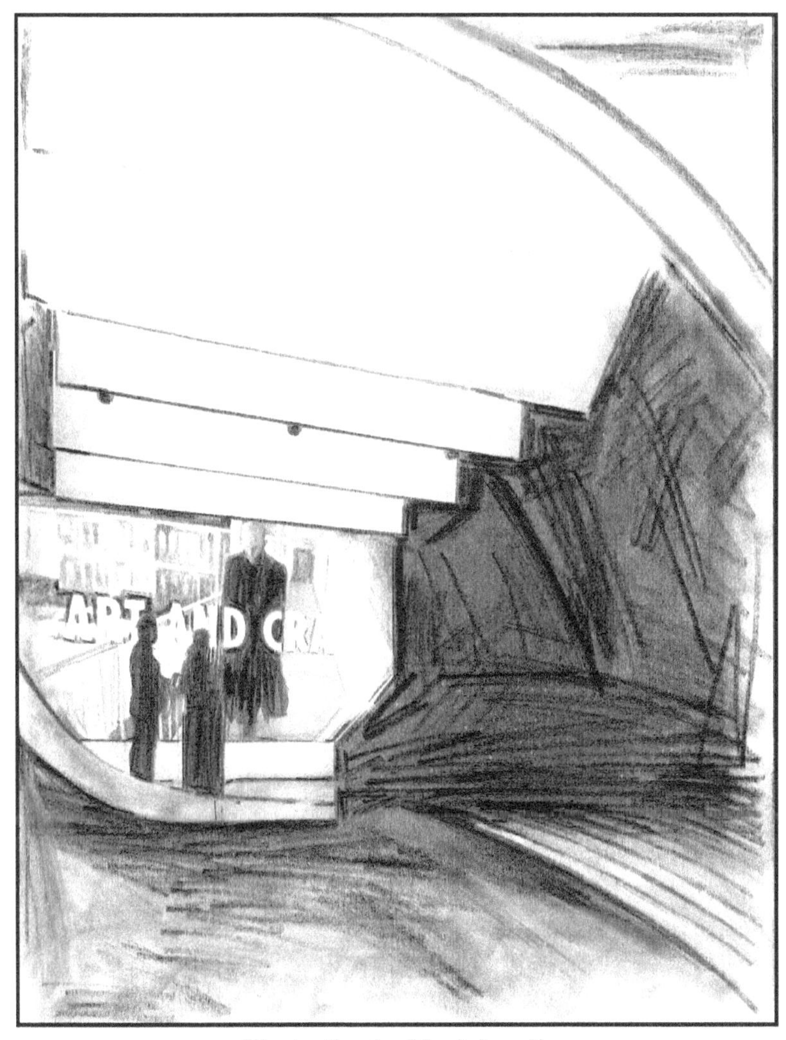

Illustration by Mark Landis

13

THE DOCUMENTARY

Before Jennifer Grausman and Sam Cullman came to make their documentary film, *Art and Craft*, some young men from the University of California, Berkeley came. They were smart, fashionable young men, in sunglasses, and it was summer and they dressed like characters in those 1980s movies with young fraternity boys getting into trouble. They came in a long limousine full of equipment. They were nice to me and I liked them, and we made friends. But they were so arrogant. Because of their demeanour I could tell right from the start it was going to be a disaster.

They swaggered in to the Lauren Rogers Museum, insolent and arrogant. I wasn't there but I can picture it. They ticked off the people at the museum and didn't get permission to film there. They spent time filming here at my apartment instead and we took drives around in Mother's car. There were three boys and a girl.

Later, they drove to Louisiana to one of the museums and tried to throw something together on film there. I never heard from them again. They were smart young men and they knew what they were doing, but it was just their attitude. If they could have been a little more mature it might have been okay. Before they arrived, I put things up on the wall to meet their expectations. Later, when Jennifer and Sam came to make their documentary, I wasn't sure what they wanted, so it was still there. If anything seemed strange or out of place it's because I put it there to meet expectations.

I believe they first contacted John Gapper at The Financial Times and he called and asked if I'd like to speak to them. When Jennifer called I told her I was flattered they wanted to make a film, but warned her I didn't do anything other than watch TV so I didn't know what they would do. When

142

Sam and Jennifer came to make their documentary they quickly became my best friends. The second time I met Sam I talked to him a while and I learned a lot. I asked him if he ever stayed friends with the men in his other films and he told me he was friends with them for the rest of their lives. I asked it loud so Jennifer could hear too. And he was right, he did stay friends with me. Mark Becker was also a director of *Art and Craft.* I never knew him quite as well.

Jennifer and Sam had the story right, but they had the wrong plot. When they came they expected there to find this frustrated genius, upset that people had laughed at his art so was seeking revenge. In "The Addams Family" there was a time when Lurch told his mother he owned the big mansion. Once they finally got rid of his mother Lurch ended up believing he *was* Mr. Addams, and he had a hard time going back to being a butler. I just wanted to impress Mother with philanthropy and then I kept doing it. It was hard to stop.

Does art imitate life or does life imitate art? The documentary *Art and Craft* was real, but we still had to do things that weren't exactly what life is like for me. My grocery store wouldn't let the film crew in—there's a lot of people—so we went to a different store than I usually shop at. Jennifer said, "It's on the expense account so just buy whatever you want," so, I bought the expensive TV dinners. I wasn't going to put a bunch of cans of Campbell's soup in there like I normally would, not when I had the chance to get the good dinners.

It reminds me of the TV show "Mad About You," where Paul Reiser's character makes documentaries. His wife Jamie Buckman (played by Helen Hunt) doesn't want their real life on camera; she wanted it to look better, so they had to keep stopping. She didn't want anyone to see they only read TV Guide. Then they just decided to have her make coffee. I make coffee in my documentary as well. I had watched Jennifer's first movie, *Pressure Cooker*, about young people in cooking school and their personal lives, and I tried to think of things for them to film. I went to places and gave things away, like at that Catholic school. I'd asked all the girls who their favorite saint was.

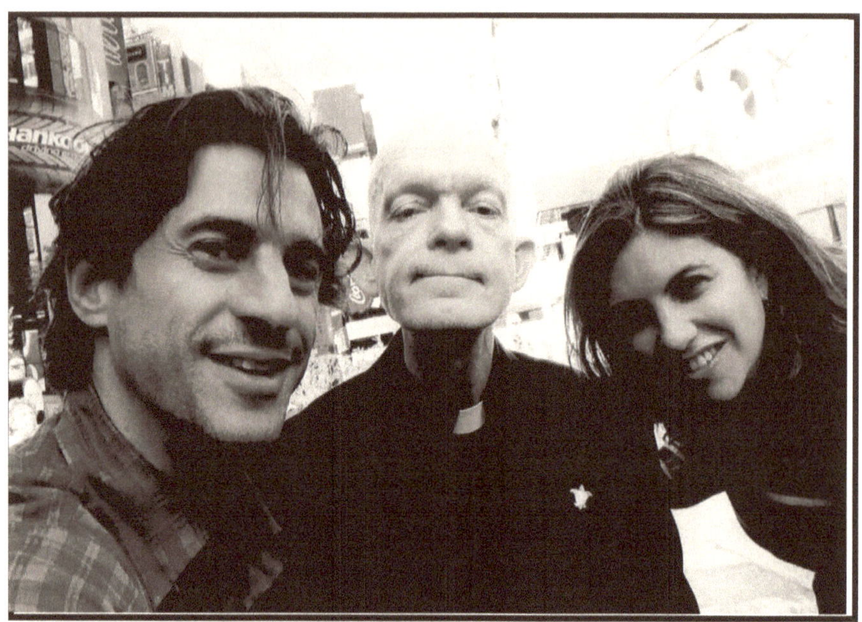

Here I am with Sam and Jennifer. Photo © Sam Cullman.

Sam and Jennifer wanted me to find paperwork and letters and needed me to go through boxes of papers. You know how you throw old receipts in with important stuff, thinking you'd need them one day, but you never do and it adds up. I lost a lot of stuff through the years because I moved a lot and I couldn't take it all, and after the hurricane I had to get rid of a lot of things then. It just didn't occur to me that fashionable filmmakers would one day show up and need me to produce things. I did my best to find the things they wanted in the film but I'm sure there was important stuff that had been thrown out that I couldn't find.

Mother would have been furious if she saw me smoking in the documentary, *Art and Craft*. She had been gone for four or five years before I started smoking. When I was a kid I was warned about smoking. I grew up with great commercials, like Johnny One Smoke who rode the range, but I remember Yul Brynner when he was dying of cancer and so nothing would have made me try a cigarette when I was young. But when I was fifty-seven, I thought, what difference does it make now?

In movies they often smoked to calm down. I'd watched *Muggable Mary*, about a woman who had a son and was struggling in New York, and he had all kinds of problems. She goes to police academy and whenever she had a close call she'd have a smoke. I had forty years of watching stuff like that. It took me a long time to learn and for the first three months I wasn't inhaling. I only tried because I was so desperate to find something to calm me down after Mother left.

When I think of the documentary I worry people think I'm still a smoker. I only did it for a year and I don't do it now. I'm a lot better than I was right after Mother died. Smoking did nothing for me, just made me feel bad and was expensive, gave me a sore throat and made me thirsty, and I quit after a year. If you don't begin until you're older it's much easier to stop. Mother took up smoking in the early 1960s to be fashionable and she gave it up when I was nine or ten and just like me, she had no difficulty quitting. Dad also smoked, and he got cancer of the throat, and died of it.

The *Art and Craft* documentary makes me cringe because I'd begun drinking brandy. I was pacing up and down on the meds I'd been prescribed and I couldn't stop. Those medications just about killed me. I took Zyprexa and some other bad ones, but Risperdal was the one that almost killed me. That's how I was driven to have my first drink. I was worried about Mother, on Risperdal, worrying about those awful relatives stealing, pacing around, up and down, like one of those caged rats, in my small room in Mother's apartment. The drinking bothers me more than anything, something I'm really ashamed of.

I blame a bunch of things. TV gave me the idea, forty years of Westerns and mostly those British movies, the Miss Marples, the ones with Margaret Rutherford, Sherlock Holmes, the great detective, English crime movies. Whenever someone is really upset it's not cigarettes they get someone, they say to get some brandy. I was watching Tess of the d'Urbervilles, because I was working my way down through the English-speaking countries and was on *Tess of the D'Urbervilles*, based on Thomas Hardy's novel. At one point, when Tess was wandering the moors, someone said to bring Tess brandy to calm her. Watching the movie gave me the idea to go buy a bottle of brandy.

I was fifty-two and it was the first time I'd ever been in a liquor store to buy something. I didn't know what to ask for. A Vietnamese lady worked there and asked how much I wanted to spend, and I said $15 so she chose a bottle for me. I remember that day well. It helped calm me down and I stopped pacing. I used to despise when I saw people drinking. I had so little money that I'd buy a case of Campbell's Chunky soup and have a half can a day, and I used to pride myself on living like one of the saints. I didn't spend money on stuff like alcohol.

I got to go to the premiere of the documentary in New York City. I was embarrassed I was in the film, so I decided to sneak out. I thought I'd just pretend I was going to the bathroom, but I'd go walk around the block until it was over; but a man came up to me in the hall and wanted to talk and it turned out he was the composer. So, we stayed and talked, and then the film started. If he hadn't been a musician he would have had a calling as a negotiator because before I knew it he'd talked me into going inside. The music was fantastic and reminded me of *The Pink Panther*.

I was slumped down so low in my seat because of embarrassment that my back hurt. I missed a lot of it visually from being crouched down, but I heard all of it. I never know if I should tell people about the film. I don't know if they'd like me in it. But I just let the filmmakers do what they wanted when they made it. They're my best friends. Really, I've made a great many friends after the film. They found my social worker I hadn't seen since she was in her twenties and now we talk again. They had to find people who knew me and that was hard for them.

At the 2014 premiere of the documentary they wanted me to come up on stage for the third showing. I'd never been on a big stage before, but I brought the house down in New York. People asked about the experience and I said that it was "Mark's big adventure" and everyone laughed. You never know a hidden talent could come up, but I learned I could do stand-up. I was fifty-nine.

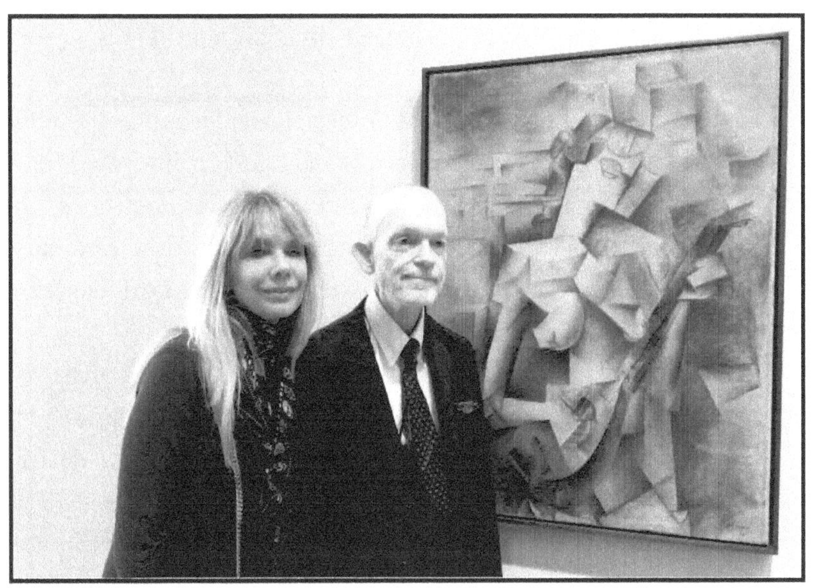

Museum of Modern Art with actress Rosanna Arquette. © Sam Cullman.

When I went to Houston for the film festival they treated me like royalty. When Mother first died I discovered YouTube and I spent a week watching all the Russian movies, even the ones without subtitles. As luck would have it, the girl running the festival was a Russian immigrant. She was particularly impressed I watched those movies, and I became friends with her and later she sent me Russian art supplies. You wouldn't think a week watching movies would be of any use to you, but I ended up making a friend for life. Dad would have been proud. Sitting around in a group home it never would have occurred to me I'd one day be getting off a plane and being met by two Russian models who would make me king for a day and remain friends with me.

When I was headed to Milwaukee and Memphis I didn't know Amazing Randy would be on the same circuit as me with his film *An Honest Liar*. I had painted the filmmaker, Justin, in 2014 as well as his wife and daughter. The Amazing Randy was a great man. He used to say, "Honesty is the best policy if the policy is honest." It's a good movie although they tried to crowd too much into it in ninety minutes. We also went to Washington where they showed my film, and it was my only standing ovation.

Sam and Jennifer have stayed my friends. I usually only pay attention to things that are of immediate concern to me, but I finally voted for the first time because Jennifer and Sam told me to. Sam recommended I stay off social media because it just wastes your time, and I listened to him. I do have a Twitter account because you sometimes get extra entries for contests if you have an account.

I did scare Sam and Jennifer a few times, through no fault of my own. They worry I will sign things after what happened, and they always look out for me. A good friend from the Art Institute in Chicago when I was twenty-one, came out of the woodwork in 2014 right after *Art and Craft* debuted. I remember I had written his term paper for him. He sent me some things in a Big FedEx box and he kept pressuring me to sign them and get them notarized, but no one signs all those things.

Eventually I signed something that said he was my manager, but I thought he was just kidding around. I thought he'd printed it off at an office supply store or bought a blank copy there. I didn't even read it. It probably wasn't legal anyhow. I remember talking to him on the phone and suggested I just sign it and he could take it to get it notarized; but he got angry and said he wanted it done right. I didn't realize he'd hired an attorney.

Jennifer and Sam were so upset when they heard but they took it to their lawyer, and he said it wasn't real. Now I show them things before signing anything. I haven't forgotten what that friend did and when he calls I never answer the phone. Because of him a film company that wanted to make a movie about me had to wait five years to be sure the contract had expired, even though it wasn't real.

I enjoyed the attention I received after the film. Everybody likes attention, and older people crave it, and certainly everyone's favorite subject is themselves. A journalist wrote a story about me and took a photo of me with a picture of the Mona Lisa hiding in my coat. The photo was my idea and I think it was a great one. He was supposed to be writing for

GQ, a responsible magazine, but after he'd written it, they turned it down and it ended up in a trashy magazine I don't subscribe to.

I read a few articles about me. There were always errors. One article claimed I said "damn" in an interview, and another said I used the word "ain't." I might be repetitive in my figure of speech, but I certainly don't use words like those.

Because of the film, actress Rosanna Arquette and I became friends. It turned out she was a fan. Sam made me go talk to her. She favored me with a bunch of communications, and we spent a day together. She ended up taking me to a museum gift store and let me fill up a shopping bag of things. I had seen her in *Mom and Dad Can't Hear Me* when I skipped class at the Chicago Institute to watch the after-school special. She was in some kind of YouTube show—I think it was called "Sideswiped*"* or something like that, and in this one she plays a mother—a glamorous mother of course—and the premise is the comedy stuff that comes with Tinder. I had never heard of Tinder until Roseanna told me about it.

I got a large check when we went around with Jennifer and Sam for the NEA to talk to students, and I stayed at fancy hotels. When I went back to Chicago I stayed in the same hotel as I did the first time. I told them I wanted everything to be as close to the way it was in 1974 when I went from the Menninger Clinic to see the school. They were real good to me, gave me a big gift basket. I think some of the furniture is the same. This time I had a better view though.

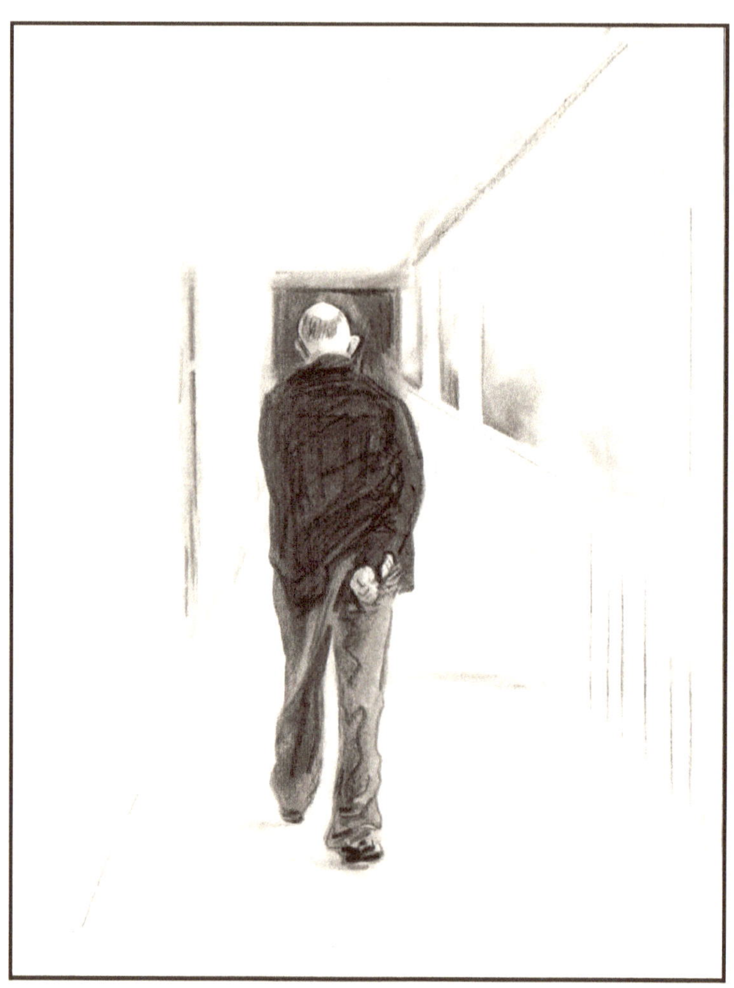

Illustration by Mark Landis

<u>14</u>

LIFE IN LAUREL

I moved back to Mississippi permanently after the hurricane in 2005, but I've been in and out of the area since 1986. After living in San Francisco I found it quite different living in Laurel again. People often mention how pretty Laurel is, but it's lost on me. I gather it is quite picturesque, but I've just lived here a long time, so one tends to overlook what visitors might notice. There is perhaps someone in Paris, France watching "In the Heat of the Night," where every week there was excitement in a small Southern town, and they may think it would be interesting and exciting to live in Mississippi, whether it's fashionable or not. There are certainly notable people from here. Eudora Welty grew up in Jackson—she and William Faulkner are the most illustrious writers— as well as Willie Morris, the man who wrote *My Dog Skip*.

It would never have occurred to me I'd end up still living in Mother's apartment, but moving would likely be the end of me. There's just too much stuff ... my collections, all of Mother's antiques... I've painted every picture on the walls, except Grandfather's portrait. I still have all of Mother and Dad's furniture. I have a plant that was only alive for a short while after Mother died because I didn't know how to take care of it but it's sitting there ten years later because it has a nice pot.

I have an easel that was a gift, but I cannot use it because my small bedroom is too crowded. It makes a nice showpiece. Much of Dad's things are no longer here. I don't remember when Mother gave his things away because I was in a hospital at that time. His neckties were from the 1960s and not fashionable anyhow, and Mother would have cared about that. But I still have Dad's Saville Row overcoat, and I still wear it. Dad wore a Cartier watch, and he had a Hamilton as well, which I wore for a while, but someone stole it. Dad's Cartier is too good so I wouldn't have the nerve to wear it. It keeps military time. On occasion I like to go into the storage room upstairs and look around because I find something new all the time.

Right after Mother died people wanted me to have a maid but I didn't like the idea of having someone in here cleaning. It makes me think of Robert Carlyle in *French Revolution,* who stacked his novel by the chair and the maid threw it away and he had to rewrite it. I didn't want anyone throwing out my things.

Mrs. Wyndham was a woman who lived in Laurel, just a couple blocks away, and she was really good to me. She befriended me in 2011 after Mother left and she did a great deal for me. She'd cater birthday parties for me or had me over to her birthday. She didn't like for me to call her Bunny, which was her name to her friends, so I usually didn't call her anything at all. She would often have me come over to get meals, including her biscuits. Her maid, Miss Dot, was famous for making a delicious pound cake. I was always getting phone calls to pick one up; sometimes they'd leave it on the swing for me.

Mrs. Wyndham liked very few people, but I could do no wrong after I was written about in The New Yorker and she was mentioned. Friends of hers called her saying that they'd read it and that did a lot for her. She liked Mother, too. Otherwise, she was quite difficult and if she didn't like someone it was no reflection on them.

Miss Dot worked for Mrs. Wyndham for forty to fifty years and they more or less lived together after Mr. Wyndham was gone. When I think of either of them today, I still picture them together. Miss Dot was opinionated and had to have her way and she often thought she was the boss. They were both strong-willed. Mrs. Wyndham had me paint a small portrait of Miss Dot because she was so fond of her. Dr. King spoke at the church in 1967 and Mrs. Wyndham had a portrait of him, and she put Miss Dot's painting next to it. In the last six months of her life, they had a fight and that was the end of Miss Dot. It's awful to have a falling out after all those years. On the TV show "Home Town," when they were renovating the Wyndham house they found Miss Dot's pound cake recipe taped inside the cabinets. They left it there on the cupboard door for the new owners when they re-did the kitchen, part of the house's history.

I gave Miss Dot Mother's clothes. It was ridiculous what Mother spent on clothes—the storeroom upstairs was full of them and a lot of the clothes were nearly new, and some still had press marks on them. I had to take so many trips that it took me ages to give them away. I had to stand on Mother's filing cabinet in the closet to reach for them and the top kind of caved in. The last thing I ever went out and did with Mother was buying clothes. She asked my opinion on shoes—something she'd never done before. A few days later she was gone.

There is a well-known actress from Laurel named Parker Posey. She has a twin brother who is a lawyer and her father owned Posey's Chevrolet. After she was graduated from high school in Laurel, she left for college and then Hollywood, where she appeared in many films, including *Scream 3*, with Courtney Cox and Neve Campbell, and *Superman Returns*. As this is being written, she is on location filming an episode of the hit streaming series, "The White Lotus," scheduled to be released in 2025. *Time* magazine has labeled Parker "Queen of the Indies," because of her many films.

One day Parker's aunt called and commissioned me to do a portrait of Parker's beloved dog, Gracie. When Parker came home for Christmas we were introduced and became friends. I must have told her about my affection for the movie, *The Heart is a Lonely Hunter* because when she returned home she wrote me a nice letter and told me she had read the book by Carson McCullers on which the movie was based. I had read the book in high school because in the early 1970s VCRs were not something I was aware of, and I didn't know if I'd ever see the movie again and I wanted to know more about it. Teenagers then didn't have the internet and weren't as sophisticated as they are today.

***

Alec Wilkinson from The New Yorker spent almost a week with me when he was writing his article. I found myself rather tired in the evenings, so Mrs. Wyndham took care of entertaining him afterwards. He took

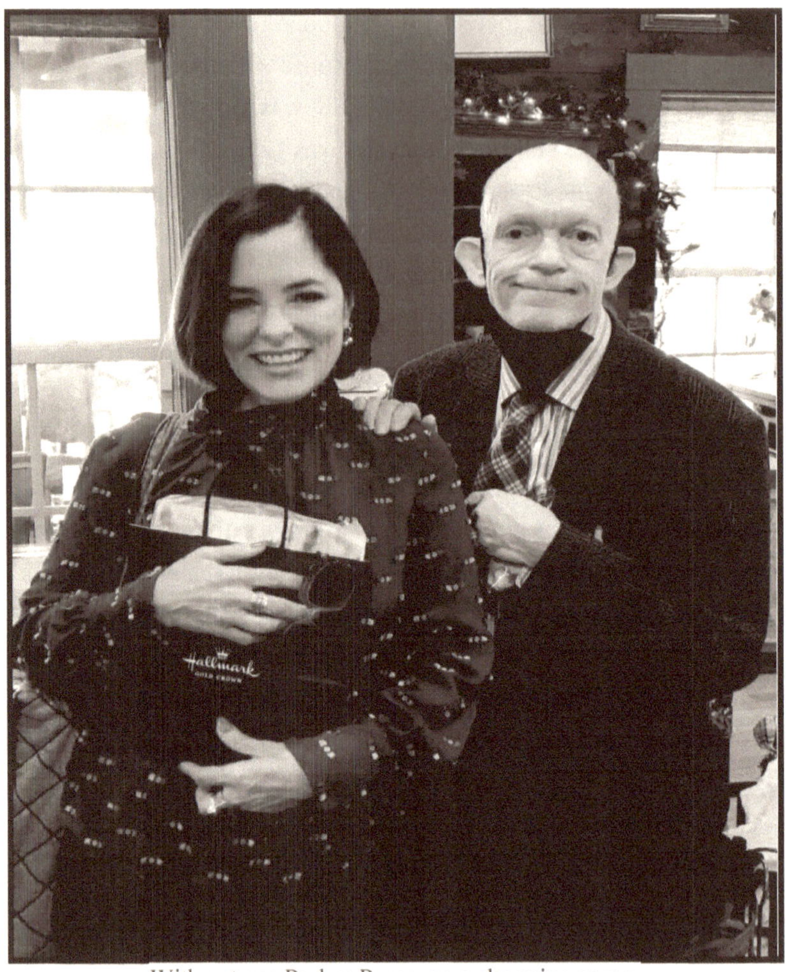

With actress Parker Posey on a shopping spree.
Photo taken with Mark Landis' camera by a bystander.

advantage of that time by interviewing people. Like all small towns, there's a good deal of gossip in Laurel, so I learned in a roundabout way that the museum director and Alec went off to a bar to discuss me, and I think that's where Alec got a lot of his info for the article.

Laurel is turning into Martha's Vineyard now, with lots of tourists and businesses that rely on them. The only close friend I have in town is Jacqueline Parker who runs the gallery, J Parker Reclaimed. Missy Brame, who manages my website and is also a good friend lived here, but recently she moved out of state. We still visit. She's a therapist and you can just tell by her picture if she can't help you, no one can. I met her at an event when she bought a commissioned piece. I meet so many people, but when she came to the door to collect the painting I recognized her right away. She invited me to her house and has been an excellent friend to me ever since. She took over my website when my friend Colette got too busy.

Dr. Colette Loll runs Art Fraud Insights and she curates all my shows. She came to my apartment one time with Jennifer and Sam and that was the first time I met her. They interviewed her and we talked but they edited her out of the movie. We got along well and she's been a good friend to me. She was the one who set up my website along with some girls that work with her. Colette teaches at Johns Hopkins University, has been a curator, and an FBI consultant and works with their art crimes department. I remember she helped with an art crime in our area involving the work of Clementine Hunter. Her brother was the chief of the Los Angeles FBI office.

Everyone else in town are friendly acquaintances. Even so, my 65th birthday was a social event and was on the front page of the newspaper. Mother would have been impressed. I don't remember having any birthday parties as a child because we were moving all the time, although I remember going to some.

When Jennifer and Sam first began filming it was my fifty-seventh birthday, I believe. We were at the Young Women's Christian Association (YWCA) where Mother had been president. Her photo that had been taken when she was seventeen was hanging in the hallway. We were going there to speak to the president, to talk about when Mother had been president. It seemed to me we were just going to have lunch there but they gave me a surprise birthday party. My former social worker Donna came—I hadn't seen her in thirteen years—but they wanted her in the film. We were sitting there, when all of a sudden high school girls came out carrying a cake and singing "Happy Birthday." It was really nice, and a memorable day for me. Afterwards I showed one of the teen girls Mother's picture.

Nowadays I keep busy. Sometimes I run over to Jacqueline's gallery and meet people if they buy one of my paintings, and I inscribe the back. The first painting I ever sold at Jacqueline's Gallery was Anne of Green Gables. I'd seen a painting of a girl and her mother making a pie with green apples in American Heritage Magazine and I thought it would make a great Anne of Green Gables. I already had a frame it would look nice in. I like people to use their imagination, and I didn't want her to look like Pippi Longstocking so I made my own version.

One day I ran over to the gallery for some reason, delivering something probably, so I visited with Jacqueline for a bit. While she was on the phone, I was sitting at the window at the same time a family was looking in. I waved at them and they recognized me so I opened the door to tell them the gallery was closed. It was a nice family from Memphis, and I talked to them about one thing after another. I told them Jacqueline would get mad at me if I opened the door for them. I'd let someone in before who'd inflicted their life story on us for ages. For some reason I did let them in but told them they had to at least buy something for $30. They ended up buying a $500 painting.

One thing that really impressed me is that they were familiar with the Brooks Museum of Art in Memphis. They despised Graceland, and they knew about the collection in the Brooks Museum, which has a Renoir, and many artists who aren't household names, like Canaletto and Gilbert Stuart, Bouguereau. They were people who wouldn't have normally impressed you as particularly sophisticated.

When I was at the film festival in Memphis, all kinds of sophisticated people asked if Jennifer and Sam wanted to go to Graceland. Michael Lehmann, the director who did the movie *Heathers,* was on the bus with us. I don't blame him and other successful, obviously talented and well-educated people, for wanting to go. Michael talked about the stress of making movies in Tinseltown, which is true, and Graceland would be a distraction. The only reason I went along was to spend as much time as I could with Sam and Jennifer, but I found it tacky, tawdry, cheap entertainment. And there I was, all this time later, in Jacqueline's gallery with a family from Memphis and they felt that way, too. They were very fine people.

I get bored and frustrated, but not lonely. I assume that if you have a sister or brother you're not used to being alone. When I was in the hospital in Jackson, before the Menninger Clinic, I was only seventeen and I was all alone. I got used to not having people around so I'm perfectly fine now. I've never wished I got married or had kids. It's hard enough to take care of myself so I can't imagine anything like raising a family. But everyone needs something to do. Purpose and direction, something that gives meaning, these are things I learned on Quora are important for older people, and I agree with that.

I do get out and about. Sometimes I see a lot of people, then things quiet down for me. The lady from psych checks in on me once a week. Two to three times a week someone takes to me to lunch and I bring it back with me so that covers dinner. I keep things I can microwave on the other days. Customers and friends may take me out, perhaps taking me to a store to get more paints. Some days I sit around and catch up on things.

I don't have a regular routine, and there's no telling when I'm up and about. Some days I'm up as early as 3:00 a.m. and take a nap later. I sleep a few hours here and there, with brief naps and it adds up to the usual six or seven hours. It's been many years since I slept all night. I get my mail at 2:00 or 3:00 in the morning so I don't need to talk to people. If I run into someone I may have to listen to their history of many surgeries or they might go on and on about all sorts of things. I feel guilty people want to hear about my life story because other men would give their pensions to talk to someone.

I can get all keyed up at night and can't sleep. I want to sleep but I'm shaky, so I get up and get all kinds of things done when I have bursts of creative energy One night a long time ago there was something I was curious about and one thing led to another and I ended up on Quora, and now sometimes I click on it and see what people are talking about. Everyone has a story.

My life would be very different if Jennifer and Sam hadn't discovered me. I've met a lot of interesting people because of them, like a filmmaker in Florida named Vinnie Taranto. He is one of the finest, bravest gentlemen and I admire him. I painted him and made him look like a hero. I've met a great many interesting people since the documentary aired.

When I was very young, nineteen or twenty, I wondered if when I was a senior I'd be a lonely old man, in a cheap hotel room, sitting on the edge of the bed, with a window and neon lights flashing outside, and with one of the letters in 'hotel' fallen down. The idea didn't necessarily bother me, but it did seem possible.

Who would have thought one day I'd sit behind Clint Eastwood at the National Board of Review Awards. There were all kinds of people there, like Meryl Streep, but it's not socially appropriate to go up to people at those sorts of functions to get autographs. You're just not supposed to behave like that, and celebrates are just people anyway.

I don't dwell on things. Your life is determined by chance. Destiny is a little too deep, and it sounds like something people in California would have pushed in the 1960s. Education and things like that matter, and who your parents were etcetera, but in the end chance matters. Everyone can say *Gee, wish I'd bought Haloid Xerox in '59 when it was 1 and ¾* and stuff like that, or *if only I'd taken the right turnoff to stop disaster*. But I don't believe in time travel stories because it's like the "Outer Limits" episode, you change the slightest little thing and everything is different. So, who knows what else might have been different if I'd made any other choices? If I thought logically and sensibly, I'd be different, and whatever flaws I might have I wouldn't have met the friends I have now. But Jennifer read an article about me and here we are. Time and chance our lives determine.

Art doesn't imitate life. People imitate TV. When people speak to me I can't help but notice things I know they picked up on TV. I know of one person who acts like the oldest boy on "Grace Under Fire." In my case, I tend to say, "you know" a lot, and I think I must have picked it up from a cartoon. I do think my life would be different if I hadn't seen certain programs. They change who you are, especially the ones you see when you are young, or the shows or episodes you know by heart. Some things are just so familiar they change who you are. When people ask if I want wine I always order a sweet wine called 'Sauternes' because they always ask for it in the movies. Seeing it on TV determined what I order.

Nowadays there's always way too much to do or nothing. On the National Board of Review channel, I've watched everything. Sam and Jennifer gave me a subscription to the Criterion Channel as a birthday present and it's full of old movies, so I make good use of it and watch that a lot. I like movies from when I was relatively young, as they bring back memories and put me in a reverie, or I watch movies from before 2000. Usually if movies have a rating of seven or above on IMDB they're worth watching. I know it's subjective, so it's not guaranteed, but you only have so much time in a day and you need a way to tell what's worth watching.

Sometimes you have to be suspicious of high ratings. You might see a strange little film with an extravagant rating but only ten people had watched it. There are times I watch a film that people have gone on about, but I find the story is ridiculous. I spend the entire time thinking it's funny people enjoyed it. All of the movies on PBS, the Agatha Christie and Miss Marple movies, they are all better than the books which are just puzzles. I don't usually watch horror films—they're not literature—but I like *Susperia*. It's a genius film, a masterpiece. You haven't seen a scary film until you've seen it. It has really good music and the coloring on it is beautiful.

I've watched a number of films with commentaries. I watched *Night of the Living Dead* on Criterion. The actor who played the hero was interviewed and he said college classes will teach that the film is a commentary on civil rights because the hero was African American, but they just hired him because he was the best actor for the part. He was a good actor, the price was right and he brought his own lunch. If they'd intentionally tried to make a socially conscious statement the movie may not have been any good; it worked because they weren't trying. I watched *Monterey Pop*—I knew the director of the movie—and I was surprised to see him. I've so often met people and don't know anything about them at the time, and I was impressed he made it because it was on TV all the time.

I'm glad I lived long enough for the Internet. Kids nowadays must be so well informed because of computers; they'd know things I wouldn't know until I was thirty. Because of the Internet I've watched episodes of shows I haven't seen since 1978. The show "The Big Blue Marble" is how I spent my Saturday mornings when I was twenty-three. I liked the featurettes. I can re-watch people interviewed and then look them up now to see if they realized their dreams. I look up actors from old TV shows on the internet to see what they've done, if they've written a book or died of a drug overdose. I like to see what happened to them.

There is no such thing as useless learning and it's wonderful that I can find out things so easily. When I was young things were just a mystery to me. If I'd see someone in an old movie I'd wonder about them and what happened to them, or if I read a passing reference to someone in a book I'd want to learn more, so it's a great luxury that I can research anything. There's more information now, but I wonder if it means there's less learning. When I was younger if I had time I'd go to the library and take a little notebook to do my research. Even then they might not have the reference book I required.

There's so much to watch on TV nowadays it's bewildering. Sometimes I can't make up my mind. I never can just watch TV; I have to be doing something, reading or painting, which can help a person feel less ashamed of wasting time. If it's a trashy show you don't feel guilty if the book is well-written because it's a profitable use of your time. I've always done that. I did homework with TV too, ever since I got one for my birthday as a teenager. "Get Smart" was my favorite show. I couldn't warm to "Happy Days" or "Three's Company."

When I used to go to the library I'd stick to the new book section, so I ended up reading lots of new things, but with TV I fall into the trap of only watching old shows, even though there is probably lots on that is great. I have nothing against contemporary shows and movies, it's just reassuring to watch things that are familiar. It's comforting. I'm not the only person my age who must feel this way.

In the Hattiesburg Mississippi Library they have a picture I gave them in the children's section. I used to go once or twice a month. The library has been a good friend to me since 1989. The original building isn't used any more. They built a much bigger one a decade ago and they turned the old one into an arts building. I like reading biographies written beautifully, ones that are very elegant. A book I really, really liked was a memoir of growing up called *Life with Father*. It's about a boy growing up and his father is a stockbroker in the 1980s and 1990s in New York. His memories seem real, nothing dramatic. Usually when I'm describing something to people I can refer to situation comedies and everyone knows what I mean, but no one might know the book if I compare it to that. Things always fail when you have to describe them.

I can't take walks for exercise and have to have a reason to walk, a need to get someplace. Before I moved to Laurel I would walk all over the place for hours because I didn't have a car and with buses you had to wait for an hour. I always thought if I paced around at a bus stop for an hour I could just walk instead and more or less be there in the same amount of time. I have nowhere near as much energy as I used to. When I was forty, I felt like thirty. But now I don't even feel like I did three or four years ago, and it seems I'm going downhill, which is just what happens as you get older. When I was in my twenties I don't think I even got common courtesy. Now I get treated with more respect and deference. Generally, I like being old, just not feeling old.

Thanks to Jennifer and Sam I stay very busy, I paint a lot of pictures and I get better all the time. Who knows how good I'll get eventually? I'm kind of getting sick of painting because I'm asked to do so much. It's taking a lot out of me and it's turning into work. Now I sell five to ten paintings a week. It used to be five to ten a year. I paint like an assembly line; I have my grandfather's genes and I'm always thinking of ways to save time. Not only do I not need to keep cleaning the brush but this method also prevents me from wasting paint or mixing colours. I do everything in that color group and then go to a different painting and use the same color group and then go back to the original I was working on.

If I squeeze too much out, I'll even wander into Mother's bathroom to see what unfinished paintings are in there. I make practical use of paint. I might have five paintings on the go at a time. I don't waste paint because I'm still not used to having any money. In many ways things stay the same. I ordered a suit, 38 regular, twenty years ago and it still fits me. It's better for me to keep being the way I've always been, careful with money and extravagances.

If there is only one piece of advice I would give to young people it's this: It's better to not be paid for something that took a couple of hours to do, than to not be paid for something that took weeks. When I thought the lady stiffed me on the large painting when I was in my twenties, it was devastating to be treated like that, and it forever changed how I paint. Experience is the best teacher, although often the hardest. It's better not to spend two weeks doing a painting, and this has been my guiding principle since I was in my twenties.

Good tools make the work faster. But I don't spend a lot of money on art supplies. Some of my brushes are twenty years old. If there's a sale I'll get a package of brushes, but I've never bought the best stuff. I still have the pastels from Woolworths from when I was twenty-one. It's very crowded in my bedroom, with old books stacked on the floor, and a big bookshelf with more books, but I have always worked in small rooms or apartments so I make do. I use an old folding chair as an easel and it's next to my television so I can listen while I'm painting. I often say: *If MacGyver were an artist, he would work like me.*

I paint almost every day. With commissions I will sometimes talk to people about what they want me to paint, but more often than not if I make decisions they don't disagree with me. I can usually tell if a painting is done if the client says it's okay, although sometimes I think of things after and add to it. I painted my own version of Starry Night for someone. I just hacked it out. Copying paintings tends to just be a puzzle to sort out. When I'm commissioned I don't care if someone asks for a masterpiece or sends a photograph of their family. You have no idea how difficult either will be. You can't read their minds so sometimes with personal photos they'll say the dog's fur is fluffier or their hair isn't the right color. You just take care of it and that's that.

If it's a copy of something you don't know how accurate they want it at first. People don't realize when you expand a small painting detail deteriorates but I'll make clients happy and add more refined things for them. There's not anything new in art. Right now, I'm working on Rembrandt's painting Sea of Galilee, an 80 by 48 inch canvas. It's just a basic composition known at the time. Some artists are struck by inspiration, but mostly art is formulaic, which is why it's easy for me. I never take a break, even if I don't want to paint something. At my age I've already done it, but I don't know I have it in me to say I can't take a commission and I also remember when I had nothing to do.

I don't really think about art in general. Every so often I see some bad art and I think that I could draw better than that in nursery school, but I don't think of myself as an artist. I don't have a style of my own; I'm not that ambitious. I'm not really much of an artist that wants to express any social concerns. A lot of modern artists are supposed to try and express things and I just wanted to be a humble commercial illustrator.

I would have liked to have been a successful commercial artist but I lacked ability and consistency. I don't follow any artists nowadays. I like painting things either I liked or Mother liked—Victorian things, academic things, cute children. I like to see what I can get away with, use up my imagination, and I like to please people. How I sign a painting varies with each one. Sometimes I carve it in and sometimes I sign things on top where there might be sky. I won't sign it across clothing or the lower part of the pictures. It's different with every painting–I just kind of know what will look all right. I'm faster than I used to be.

When I'm commissioned I like it when they give me the frame first, then I get an idea of what I want to put in it. I always tell artists to start with the frame so you know what to paint—the frame tells you what to do. If you were to say to yourself you want to read a good book, it's hard because there are an awful lot of them, but it's helpful to have an authority tell you which one. It's like that for me with frames—it gets me started. Then I won't waste any time or get confused because I just do what looks good. I began this technique early on, when one gallery would take my paintings, but I had to provide the frames, so I'd get those first for $1.00. I can buy a small frame for a quarter a piece and can replace the picture. Portraits of children look better in small frames, I think, and large frames just aren't appropriate.

I go to the Salvation Army to look for the frames. I get books there now, too. Mother would be so upset I shop there and would probably say, "What if somebody saw you?" Yet, I met a lady with a fashionable chic house on the coast, built in the 1940s but real space-age, like on "The Jetsons," and she said she managed to fill it up with lots of things from the Salvation Army, like old furniture. I did a benefit once for the Salvation Army.

It's best not to worry about what other people will think of your art. If you start worrying about opinions you'll be afraid of going through a doorway. The best things written, painted, or composed, the artists didn't stop and ask what the boys in the legal department think—they just had a burst of inspiration and went with it. Artists shouldn't worry about political correctness or hurting someone's feelings or what people will think—just do it and then consider those things later.

Being born extraordinarily wealthy would be an advantage in life in general, but you don't always use your creativity and intelligence. Sometimes in Tinseltown they have a lot of money to make a film, but the movie is a disaster. Yet an Indie filmmaker with very little money makes something creative and extraordinary. When I was young I was sometimes resentful, and wished I had money like other young people, but money is a disadvantage to artists. Not having money forces you to be creative.

Jacqueline has sold so many of my paintings that I can buy myself a few things. I recently bought holy cards on the auction from eBay from Portugal, Spain, and France and I keep them all together in a box. Some are quite old and expensive, but even the cheaper ones are really nice. I keep my best ones on lace in a different box. I always wanted to be a famous art collector, but I collect things I can afford, like stamps and children's books.

I like to autograph things, framed movie stars like Helen Slater, something that prints out nicely from a book that had a really good photograph. Often, I will take a page or two out and autograph them in the usual way…. whatever looks good in a frame. I very much like to do inscriptions. I used to be able to get nice old books by authors like Faulkner and Hemingway for 25 cents at Goodwill. I remember one time the Laurel Jones County Library threw out a lot of old children's books. Some of them were quite old, from the 1960s. I collected a bunch of them and got rid of all the stuff that identified them as being from the library. I disguised the dates real cleverly by doing children's doodles and I had a good time. I drew all kinds of things like space men and tanks, or a pretty girl, as if some little boy had a crush on somebody. Sometimes I still find myself doing it.

I like to make all kinds of other things from art and craft supplies. I make handbills and pamphlets, and replica buttons and I have them pinned on fabric and framed. I can make all kinds of things from arts and craft supplies... I remember I once made a very nice Zachary Taylor plate from 1849 for the museum in New Orleans. I like to repair dolls and religious statues, too. I have a statue that's bronze that I bought at an auction on the internet. It was missing all its fingers and I repaired it with plasticine and then painted it. You'd never know it was broken. I look for stuff that's damaged because it's cheap and then I regularly use modelling clay, acrylics and paint to fix it. You'd be surprised what you can do; you just can't handle it afterward.

There are a lot of dolls in the apartment but only one belonged to my family. Mother didn't collect them. I bought them for myself to repair, but then got attached to them. I do have figurines of Mother's, and a doll under glass, one of the few things I have of my grandmother's (Dad's mother).

Sometimes I overhear people talking about travel, and I read about it on Quora. You can subscribe to things you're interested in, and I put travel, so I read lots of horror stories, about all the things that can go wrong when you travel, all the perils. There is no place I want to travel to now, and I just don't understand why people would travel for pleasure. I would think travelling in books is the best way to travel. It's not dangerous and expensive. You can travel back in time when you read history books. I used to love the Robert Osborne travel logs, the 1940s animation where they humanize the globe.

In 2022 I travelled to New York City for an exhibition of my work at the Salomon Arts Gallery, curated by Sabrina Wirth. Sam had been filming for a follow-up documentary about me, and he had introduced me to Sabrina over the phone, a curator and artist who is heavily involved in the art world. Later on, we met virtually by Skype. In spring of 2022 she put on a solo retrospective exhibition for me in Tribeca, and it was a very glorious success, attended to capacity. Andy Warhol would have very much approved. I was part of a talk afterwards and there was standing room only, which I very much enjoyed, and the audience enjoyed it too. The entire evening was a wonderful and glorious success, and I made many new friends and received a number of commissions for portraits. It was the happiest day and evening of my life. Needless to say, Sabrina's support is a huge lift for my self-worth, especially at this time of my life of seriously declining health.

Recently I had a trip to Massachusetts, as I had an exhibit at the Norman Rockwell Museum. I hadn't been anywhere in a long time so it became a bit of an adventure, and I stayed up at night and thought about what I'd pack and what I'd wear. I got a travelling wallet so I wouldn't be victimized by pickpockets, although I might have overdone it, preparing like I was going to some dangerous place in South America. Missy Brame went with me. My Cinderella and Red Riding Hood paintings are now in the permanent collection at the museum. It gave me a boost and lifted my self-esteem. Someone asked me if I'd ever copied Norman Rockwell. I said, "No, I hadn't. He's too difficult." That made everyone laugh. I said I

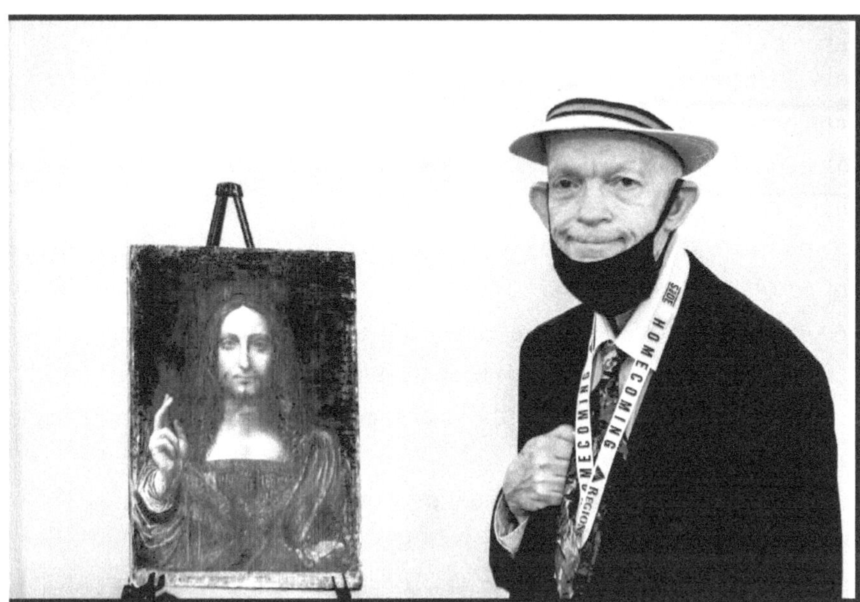

The Salvator Mundi I copied for the premiere of the documentary.
Photo by Secret Playground.

liked to do easy people like John Marin because he just did a bunch of stupid, kid-like sailboats. That also made people laugh.

There were a lot of wealthy prominent people there, and a lot of people who came out were successful illustrators, even older than me. I made friends with a couple of them. They sympathized with me. Getting things done fast before you don't get paid—that resonated with them. The people who had come out were complimentary, but they'd say things you'd expect them to say, so when illustrators took an interest I was very flattered. I would have liked to have been one.

There was recently a documentary about the Salvator Mundi—*The Lost Leonardo*—about a painting that might be a lost Da Vinci. They had me paint a copy of it for the premiere at the film festival in Birmingham. I considered it very easy to paint. After the screening I got on stage with Rachel, the creative director, when she talked about the movie. There is a scene in the movie where the man who bought the picture at auction is in New York and takes it to an art restorer and expert, and he puts it in a garbage bag. I said to the audience, "It makes sense because it was a rainy day." That made the audience laugh. I told Jennifer and Sam I did the same thing in our movie because I had a lot of things to take to Fed Ex, which also got laughs, but I wasn't trying to be funny. I just make use of household items.

I'm a better sort of person these last ten years just from the influence of people being nice to me. I don't know if hospitals helped, but I think people just improve as we get older. It's a cliché, but I just matured. My ethics have improved, and I've become more honest. I was stuffy and shy when I was in my twenties, and I've changed a lot in my personality in the last fifteen years.

Now I raise a lot of money for charities by donating paintings. I very much believe in St Jude Children's Research Hospital and the Shriners. I wish I had an opportunity to give a lot because I believe in helping charities for the sick. The photographer Diane Arbis said the disabled, people who overcome severe disabilities, are the world's true aristocrats.

I check on Jennifer and Sam every one or two weeks to see what's going on. It gives me a boost. Jennifer is like a sister. She looks out for me. We can read each other's minds and if something is bothering her, I can tell. Mother would be pleased I have so many good friends now.

Fifty years from now I'm not sure what people will think of me. I read a lot of biographies and history because I have a lot of time. George Washington was terribly worried about his reputation when he was gone, worried himself sick about it and hired biographers. He had a lofty idea of himself, but there wasn't much he could do about it.

When it comes to little people like me, I think that hopefully whatever happens when "the great veil of toil and trouble" is done, as Burmashave puts it, we will be beyond such concerns, so I'm not worried about that. Obviously when you get older you want to look back and reflect on your life and be proud. The man who invented Sea-Monkeys looks back and knows he just conned a lot of kids out of their allowance. But thanks to Sam and Jennifer telling people about me I've done a lot of nice pictures for people, all for a reasonable price.

I'd be flattered if people forge my work someday. Already paintings show up that I've forgotten about. I don't remember painting them.

Looking back at my life my only complaints are when I was well into my thirties, when the medications were added. But everything that happens in our past adds up and you can't bewail it; you wouldn't be the same if anything changed… kind of like that stuff about flapping butterfly wings. Time and chance our lives determine…

THE END

I've sometimes wondered how the young Mark Landis would have fared if raised in today's child-centric society, where Mother might have been far more likely to do crafts all day with the young boy and arrange play dates (where the other kids would no doubt be encouraged to be inclusive), where his parents would have been apt to stay at home with him in the evenings rather than go out to parties as was common for that time, and where mental health help and integration were more readily available for a child with challenges.

Would he have had more confidence in himself? Would more support have meant no group homes or bankruptcy? Would mental health supports have meant no breakdown at seventeen or stints in psychiatric institutions? Would it have meant no art forgery to impress Mother?

But as Mark often told me, our experiences make us who we are, and without them we'd be different people. Unlike me, Mark does not look back and ask himself, "what if?" Who wouldn't wish an easier life for him, yet what person who has really gotten to know him would want to see him changed? He is charming and funny, extremely intelligent, and as one of his friends said to me, "Mark tends to collect people." And strikingly, when asked about his life Mark would change very little.

To him, second-guessing and regrets are pointless exercises. He compares the human desire to question the past or worry about the future with a "Twilight Zone" episode from the 1960s, called "Nick of Time." In that episode a couple are stranded at a diner where there is fortune-telling machine. The man ends up repeatedly putting money in, trying to find out what the future holds and what he needs to do about it. In the end he is trapped in the booth forever.

"When you ask, 'what if,' 'what if,' 'what if,'… you would get trapped wondering. People get trapped never doing anything if they think too much about things, just like in the "'Twilight Zone,'" Mark told me. He laments nothing.

Despite challenges many would find insurmountable, Mark has made his way through them, keeping his sense of humor and wit intact, his compassion still strong. What I noticed most is that he is seldom angry at people, and rarely faults anyone for their behavior, typically trying to see their point of view. He admires men who are "true gentlemen," men like his father, and although Mark doesn't think he has anything in common with his dad, I would most definitely describe him as a gentleman, too.

He's a complex man. To call his donations "performance art" misses the point. Mark was never thumbing his nose at the art world, as has been said, and he truly hopes no one thinks that. The intention was not to dupe anyone as part of a social commentary on the nature of fine art. It was a means to an end: human connection. He was lonely and he found a reason for people to speak to him, to treat him with respect. As he put it, it became "addictive." It made sense to him at the time, and it still does. Truthfully, if we were all to experience a life like his, it may make perfect sense to us, too.

When we first began talking of movies and television so often, I thought perhaps reality and fiction were blurred for Mark, but I soon learned old cinema and television are just the filters through which he processes the real world, because art and life merge in so many ways. He has a keen sense of perception about many foibles of the human race and relishes comparing them to those seen on screen. He also believes we are influenced by the media we've been soaked in since we were first plunked on sofas in front of televisions or lined up for our first movies, and he often scans people to see which characters peek out, tries to discern which influences they've incorporated into their own being.

Right off the bat he informed me that I reminded him of a teacher on "The Wonder Years," ("the snappy one, the one with social activism, always a choke in her voice"). It's almost a type of game for him. And for a man of few words, descriptions of people or events can be a challenge; he told me, "It's hard enough to be articulate so if you can, reference something with TV." I have yet to find something that he *can't* find a comparison to in television. His encyclopedic knowledge of TV and cinema is uncanny. I've learned an enormous amount about classic cinema and actors from him.

Mark and I began collaborating on this book at the beginning of the COVID-19 pandemic in 2020. I had seen the wonderful documentary about him, *Art and Craft,* years earlier and was mesmerized. I love people who don't conform. After seeing an episode of the home renovation television show, "Home Town," set in his hometown of Laurel, Mississippi, I learned he was doing commissions. I hired him to paint a portrait of my husband's dog, and I got to know him a little when he had questions for me.

The early days of the pandemic were quiet and lonely for many, and it occurred to me I might write an article on him, a self-described "lonely old shut-in," but one thing led to another, and with the chasm of pandemic lockdowns looming helping him with a memoir gave us both something to do. It began as phone calls when we had time, my cell phone on speaker and me typing while he talked. Often, I'd give him a few topics or questions to mull over, and he'd jot down thoughts in a little notebook over the course of the week which he'd share at our next meeting. After about an hour he would sing an old musical number about having "teenage telephone ear" and we'd call it quits.

By spring of 2021 Mark decided we should become "disciplined" and we began having Monday Zoom meetings, never missed, the week between meetings punctuated by our frequent emails and texts. In fact, Mark was far from a "shut-in" and frequented an art gallery to sign paintings and pose for photos, which he'd send to me later. Several times a week he'd send a photo of an interesting book he'd come across or some matter or interest. He never missed connecting at a holiday. Between calls I'd give him a few questions to think about during the week and then he'd relay his answers in meandering stories.

We both really enjoyed our conversations.

"Hey, this must be what therapy feels like!" he often remarked.

He regularly mentioned how lucky he was to have someone want to hear him talk nonstop, that most seniors wished for that. I could never quite make him understand what a compelling story he had: the portrait of the artist as a young man. Nor could I convince him he was likeable and well worth talking to, that I got a great deal out of all our chats, and that I looked forward to them. He had snippets of wisdom that stayed with me and would pop in my head from time to time when I was in various situations. In time, it dawned on me that in this era of judgment, polarization, and 'cancel culture,' it behooves us all to share—and read—stories that differ from our own. Although I am mother to several children with complex special needs, listening to Mark helped me not only understand him better, but others who are socially isolated.

His story poured out, usually in circles, rather than linear, a five-minute anecdote taking ten times as long as we side-tracked into television shows, and movies. He had an unbelievable memory when it came to that and remembered details of shows he hadn't seen in thirty years. He seemed to be a database of actors' biographies, no matter how obscure they were. He also knew a great deal about world history and tended to meander onto other topics.

We blew the dust off the old photo albums and Mark said many good memories surfaced for him, once forgotten, and now happily restored. He'd wander around his apartment with his laptop, showing me every nook and cranny. He'd dig through storage in his spare time and emerge with some small treasure, a Sunday school certificate or report card. He got to know my family, usually remembering them by pairing them with an actor by the same name. He would always say, "How is your husband? Trevor, like Trevor Howard, a fine British actor…" and then go off on a tangent about wonderful films.

Sometimes my kids would stick their heads in front of the camera to have a quick chat with him when they passed by my office. He'd surprise them with a sketch in the mail or ask how they were doing. He could recognize my dogs' barks, shouting hello to Keeper or Fenwick, and knew if the mailman or my husband had arrived based on their sound. Before we knew it, we'd become good friends, as if we'd known each other for ages; in time he felt like a distant uncle, and we developed a genuine affection for him that made him feel like family. Sometimes we didn't work on the book at all and just got caught up on the week's events.

Mark was determined his memoir be factual, no embellishments or half-truths, just the most accurate account that he could recall, given the limitations of memory, which he acknowledged. Because the book was written as an interview, cut and pasted, any errors are quite likely mine. Mainly, he wanted to clear up the misperceptions he felt people had about him. He insisted that people are too often pretentious and conceited; they think they are Napoleon, and they laugh at the people they have tricked. He felt humility is the first of the virtues—and mocking anyone he'd duped wasn't his intention.

"I want a literary book people can trust, a solid piece of literature," he said and he promised he'd done his "very best to be realistic with things" when he shared his stories, even though he said they'd be more exciting if they were embellished. He wanted it to be a book like *Maria Chapdelaine*—something he mentioned often, the title said with a flourish—which unfortunately I hadn't read.

Often, as he told a story he'd say, "I'm relying on you as a writer to make this sound better." But I couldn't. Mark's voice is distinct. There had been articles written *about* him already. What was needed was his story told entirely from *his* point of view, said as though he were sitting at your kitchen table. Mark is not always a descriptive man. As he put it, "you can't describe things, you need to see them!"

To him, truly, a picture is worth a thousand words. But somehow, as we wove together his musings, Mark's life was revealed, its color, shape and form set down on the page, his literary self-portrait.

Christen Shepherd
Dorchester, Ontario, Canada

Samples of the Work
of
Mark Landis

A LARGE COLLECTION
OF HIS ORIGINAL WORK
WILL APPEAR IN THE
HARD COVER EDITION
IN FULL COLOR

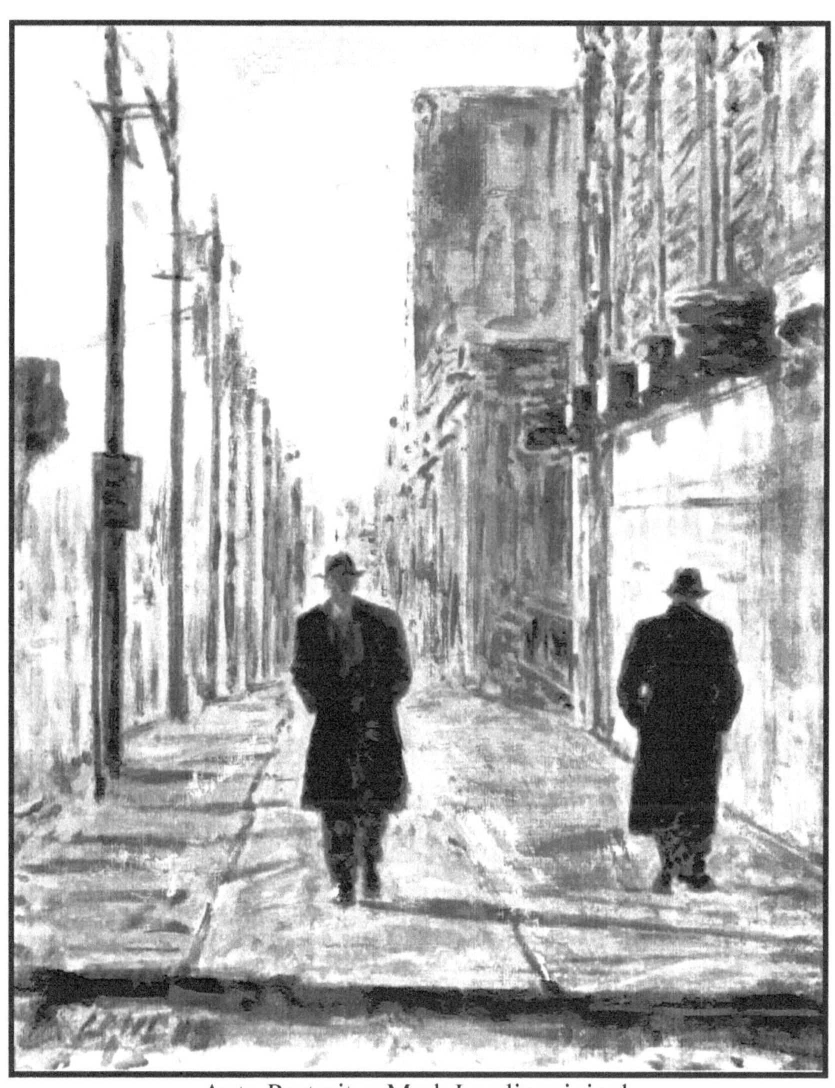

Auto Portrait, a Mark Landis original.

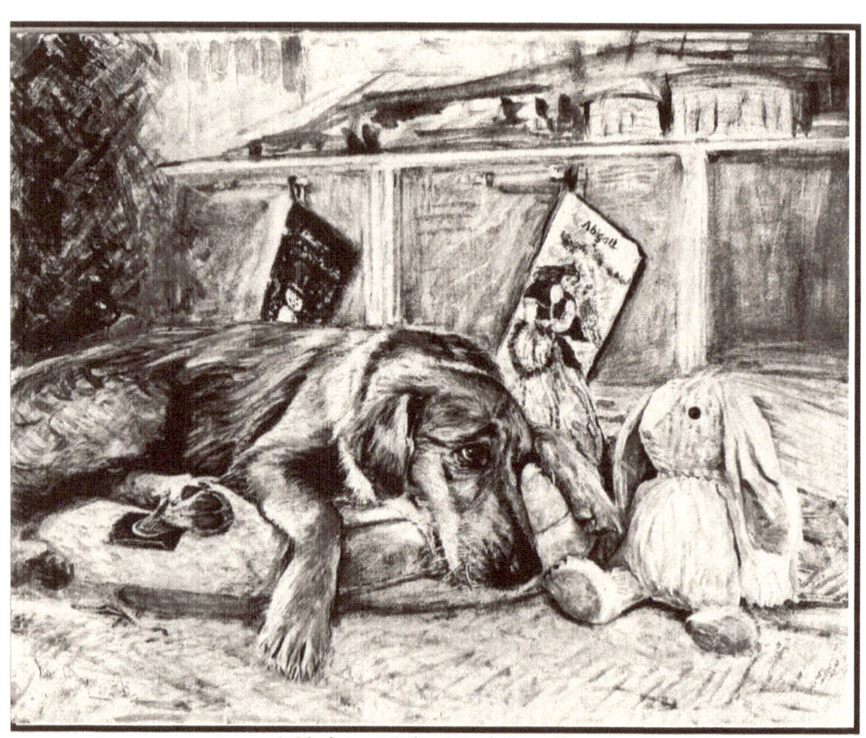

"Christmas" by Mark Landis

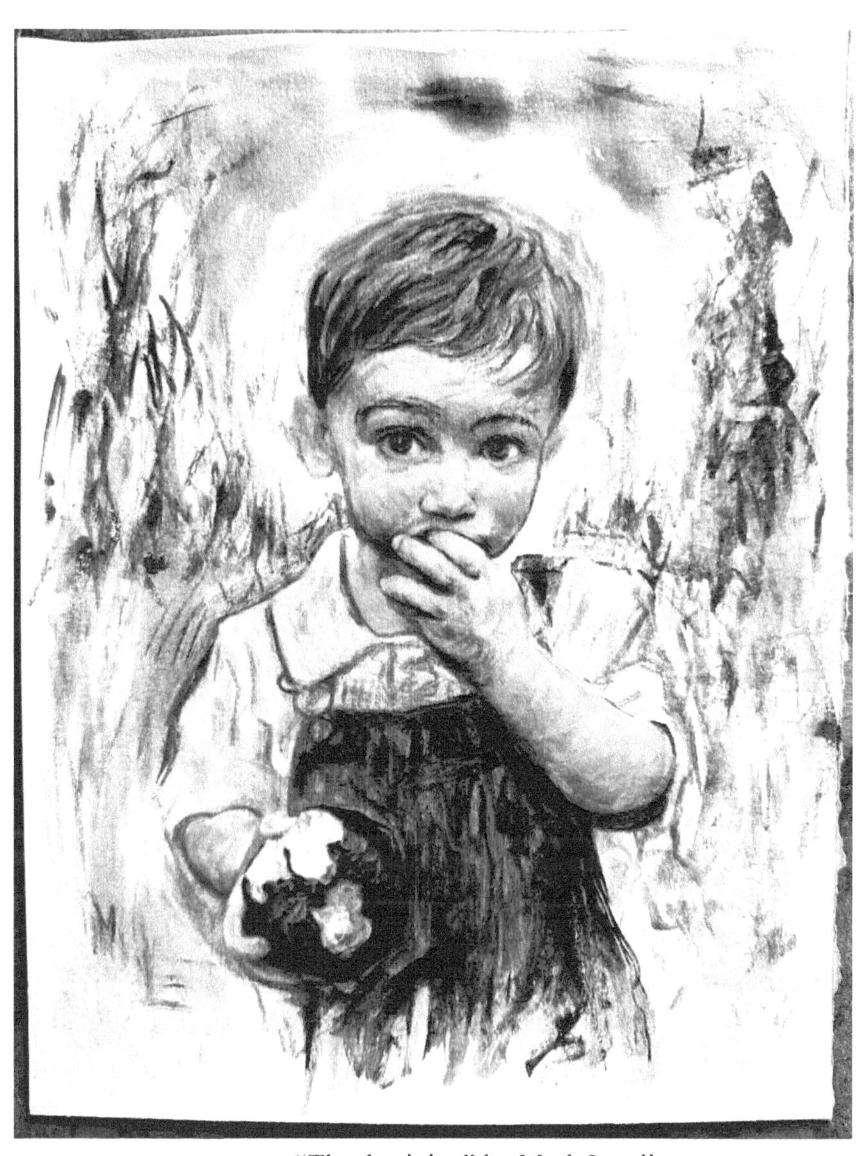

"Thanksgiving" by Mark Landis

Acknowledgments

Mark Landis

I would like to express my gratitude to my good friends: Missy Brame, Sam Cullman, Jennifer Grausman, Dr. Colette Loll Marvin, director of Art Fraud Insights, and Jacqueline Parker. I am thankful to James L. Dickerson of Sartoris Literary Group, a fine southern gentleman, for his hard work on the book. Thank you to those who have supported me or written about me over the years, including: Rosanna Arquette, Mark Becker, John Gapper, James Hutchinson, of The Glasgow College of Art, Birney Imes, editor of the *Columbus Commercial Dispatch;* Parker Posey, Alex Stone, author of *Fooling Houdini;* Aubrey Tang, PhD, Chapman University; Helene Vissiere, Alec Wilkinson, and Sabrina Wirth. I am very grateful.

Christen Shepherd

Deeply appreciative of my husband Trevor, and my children (Michael, Dermott, Zach, Serena, Sam, Livvy, Em, and Maria) for your enthusiasm and championing this project; thanks go out to my parents, Maureen Wyatt, Bob Doidge and his partner Caroline Downman, my sister Katie, in-laws, Mike and Suzanne Shepherd, cousin Corey, and the rest of my family for support. I'm grateful for the encouragement of my many wonderful friends, including Jane Barrett, Jen Bodenham, Dr. Erica Dickie, Lisa Highfield, and Nicole Smith, and my NS writers' group. Thanks to Daniel Lanois for driving home that above all, we have a responsibility to the art. Thank you to James L. Dickerson of Sartoris for truly believing Mark had a story to tell, and for his patience as we pieced together the book. Lastly, thank you to Mark Landis, for your friendship and fun over the last few years while writing this book, and for all you've taught me and all of your wisdom shared.

www.ingramcontent.com/pod-product-compliance
Lightning Source LLC
Chambersburg PA
CBHW060546160726
47991CB00001B/452